CAMBRIDGE LIBRARY COLLECTION

Books of enduring scholarly value

Art and Architecture

From the middle of the eighteenth century, with the growth of travel at home and abroad and the increase in leisure for the wealthier classes, the arts became the subject of more widespread appreciation and discussion. The rapid expansion of book and periodical publishing in this area both reflected and encouraged interest in art and art history among the wider reading public. This series throws light on the development of visual culture and aesthetics. It covers topics from the Grand Tour to the great exhibitions of the nineteenth century, and includes art criticism and biography.

An Attempt to Discriminate the Styles of English Architecture, from the Conquest to the Reformation

First published in 1817, this highly influential study by Thomas Rickman (1776–1841) provides a classic overview of English medieval architecture. A devotee of the Gothic style, Rickman forged a successful career as an architect of Anglican churches, in the face of criticism from his Quaker brethren. This study is founded on the attention to detail and delight of a true enthusiast, drawing on knowledge of some five hundred buildings across the British Isles. Describing Greek and Roman influences before delineating English architecture since the Norman Conquest, Rickman presents a compelling narrative of architectural styles and precedents. Illustrated with a number of detailed drawings, the work ends with short entries, organised by county, on notable cathedrals, churches and abbeys. Introducing terminology and classifications that are still used today, the book quickly became an essential reference work for architectural students and practitioners. This reissue is of the first edition.

Cambridge University Press has long been a pioneer in the reissuing of out-of-print titles from its own backlist, producing digital reprints of books that are still sought after by scholars and students but could not be reprinted economically using traditional technology. The Cambridge Library Collection extends this activity to a wider range of books which are still of importance to researchers and professionals, either for the source material they contain, or as landmarks in the history of their academic discipline.

Drawing from the world-renowned collections in the Cambridge University Library and other partner libraries, and guided by the advice of experts in each subject area, Cambridge University Press is using state-of-the-art scanning machines in its own Printing House to capture the content of each book selected for inclusion. The files are processed to give a consistently clear, crisp image, and the books finished to the high quality standard for which the Press is recognised around the world. The latest print-on-demand technology ensures that the books will remain available indefinitely, and that orders for single or multiple copies can quickly be supplied.

The Cambridge Library Collection brings back to life books of enduring scholarly value (including out-of-copyright works originally issued by other publishers) across a wide range of disciplines in the humanities and social sciences and in science and technology.

An Attempt to Discriminate
the Styles of
English Architecture
from the Conquest
to the Reformation

*Preceded by a Sketch of the Grecian and Roman Orders,
with Notices of Nearly Five Hundred English Buildings*

THOMAS RICKMAN

CAMBRIDGE
UNIVERSITY PRESS

CAMBRIDGE
UNIVERSITY PRESS

University Printing House, Cambridge, CB2 8BS, United Kingdom

Published in the United States of America by Cambridge University Press, New York

Cambridge University Press is part of the University of Cambridge.
It furthers the University's mission by disseminating knowledge in the pursuit of
education, learning and research at the highest international levels of excellence.

www.cambridge.org
Information on this title: www.cambridge.org/9781108066426

This edition first published 1817
This digitally printed version 2013

ISBN 978-1-108-06642-6 Paperback

PLATE XIII.

I.Rickman del.

W.Radclyffe sc.

Published by J & J. Smith, Liverpool, 1 July, 1817.

AN

ATTEMPT TO DISCRIMINATE

THE STYLES

OF

𝕰nglish 𝕬rchitecture,

FROM THE

Conquest to the Reformation;

Preceded by

A SKETCH

of

THE GRECIAN AND ROMAN

ORDERS,

with

NOTICES OF NEARLY FIVE HUNDRED ENGLISH BUILDINGS.

———

By THOMAS RICKMAN,

Member of the Literary and Philosophical Societies of Liverpool and Chester.

———

LONDON,

PUBLISHED BY LONGMAN, HURST, REES, ORME, AND BROWN, PATERNOSTER-ROW ; AND SOLD BY THE BOOKSELLERS IN GENERAL.

𝔍. and 𝔍. Smith, Printers, Liverpool.

Preface.

~~~~~~~~~~~~~~~~~~~~~~~~~~~~~~~~~

AN outline of the present essay was written by the Author for Smith's "Panorama of Science and Art," and published in that work some years ago, but having been frequently requested to enlarge and republish it, he has now performed that task, and has subjoined a copious list of buildings for the student's instruction.

The object of the present publication has been to furnish, at a price which shall not present an obstacle to extensive circulation, such a view of the principles of Architecture, more particularly that of the British Isles, as may not only be placed with advantage in the hands of the rising generation, but also afford the guardians of our ecclesiastical edifices such clear discriminative remarks on the buildings now existing, as may enable them to judge with considerable accuracy of the restorations necessary to be made in those venerable edifices that are under their peculiar care ; and also, by leading them to the study of such as still remain in a perfect state, to render them more capable of deciding on the various designs for churches in imitation of the English styles, which may be presented to their choice.

As a text-book for the architectural student, little need be said of this publication. The want of such a work, particularly as it respects the English styles, is generally acknowledged; and it has been the aim of the Author, by a constant reference to buildings, to instil the principles of practice rather than mere theoretical knowledge.

This essay is by no means intended to supersede that more detailed view of English architecture which the subject merits and requires : an undertaking of this nature must necessarily be expensive, from the requisite number of plates, without which it is impossible to give a full view of this interesting subject; but should the present work be favourably received, the Author may be stimulated, if time and opportunity be afforded him, again to intrude himself on the Public.

CONTENTS.

An Attempt, &c.

The science of Architecture may be considered, in its most extended application, to comprehend building of every kind: but at present we must consider it in one much more restricted; according to which, Architecture may be said to treat of the planning and erection of edifices, which are composed and embellished after two principal modes,

1st, the Antique, or Grecian and Roman,

2nd, the English or Gothic.

We shall treat of these modes in distinct dissertations, because their principles are completely distinct, and indeed mostly form direct contrasts. But before we proceed to treat of them, it will be proper to make a few remarks on the distinction between mere house-building, and that high character of composition in the Grecian and Roman orders, which is properly styled Architecture; for though we have now many nobly architectural houses, we are much in danger of having our public edifices debased, by a consideration of what is convenient as a house; rather than what is correct as an architectural design.

In order properly to examine this subject, we must consider a little, what are the buildings regarded as our models for working the orders, and in what climate, for what purposes, and under what circumstances they were erected. This may, perhaps, lead to some conclusions, which may serve to distinguish that description of work, which, however rich or costly, is still mere house-building, in point of its composition.

It is acknowledged, on all hands, that our best models, in the three ancient unmixed orders — the Doric, Ionic, and Corinthian, are the remains of Grecian temples. Most of them were erected in a climate, in which a covering from rain was by no means necessary, and we shall find this circumstance very influential; for as the space within the walls was always partially, and often wholly open, apertures in those walls for light were not required; and we find, also, in Grecian structures, very few, sometimes only one door. The purpose for which these buildings were erected, was the occasional reception of a large body of people, and not the settled residence of any But, perhaps, the circumstances under which they were erected, have had more influence on the rules which have been handed down to us, as necessary to be observed in composing architectural designs, than either the climate or their use. It is now pretty generally agreed, that the Greeks did not use the arch, at least in the exterior of their public buildings, till it was introduced by the Romans. Here then we see at once a limitation of the intercolumniation, which must be restrained by the necessity of finding stones of sufficient length to form the architrave. Hence the smaller comparative intercolumniations of the Grecian buildings, and the constant use of columns; and hence the propriety of avoiding arches, in compositions of the purer Grecian orders.

The Romans introduced the arch very extensively, into buildings of almost every description, and made several alterations in the mode of working the orders they found in Greece, to which they added one order, by mixing the Corinthian and Ionic, and another by stripping the Doric of its ornaments. Their climate, also, was so far different as to require more general roofing, but still, from the greater necessity of pro-

viding a screen from the heat of the sun, than apertures to admit the light, it does not appear that large
windows were in general use, and hence an important
difference in modern work. Although, by roofs and
arches, much more approximated to modern necessities than the Grecian models, still those of Rome
which can be regarded as models of composition, are
temples, or other public edifices, and not domestic
buildings, which, whenever they have been found,
appear unadapted to modern wants, and therefore
unfit for imitation.

In a few words, we may sum up the grand distinctions between mere building and architectural design:
the former looks for convenience, and though it will
doubtless often use architectural ornaments, and preserve their proportions, when used as smaller parts, yet
the general proportion may vary very widely from the
orders, and yet be pleasing, and perhaps not incorrect;
but all this is modern building, and not architecture
in its restricted sense; in this the columns are essential
parts, and to them and their proportions all other
arrangements must be made subservient; and here we
may seek, with care and minuteness, amongst the
many remains yet left in various parts, (and of which
the best are familiar to most architectural students,
from valuable delineations by those who have accurately
examined them,) for models, and in selecting and
adopting these, the taste and abilities of the architect
have ample space.

As an introduction to the dissertations, it may not
be amiss to take a hasty sketch of the progress of
Architecture in England.

Of the British architecture, before the arrival of the
Romans in the island, we have no clear account; but
it is not likely it differed much from the ordinary
modes of uncivilized nations; the hut of wood with
a variety of coverings, and sometimes the cavities of
the rock, were doubtless the domestic habitations of
the aboriginal Britons; and their stupendous public

edifices, such as Stonehenge and others, still remain to us. The arrival of the Romans was a new era; they introduced, at least in some degree, their own architecture, of which a variety of specimens have been found; some few still remain, of which, perhaps, the gate of Lincoln is the only one retaining its original use. Although some fine specimens of workmanship have been dug up in parts, yet by far the greatest part of the Roman work was rude, and by no means comparable with the antiquities of Greece and Italy, though executed by the Romans. The age of purity, in the Roman architecture, reaches down to several of the first emperors, but very early with a degree of purity of composition, there was such a profusion of ornament made use of, as soon led the way to something like debasement of composition. The palace of Dioclesian, at Spalatro, has descended to us sufficiently perfect to enable us to judge of the style of both composition and ornamental details; and the date of this may be considered from A. D. 290 to 300; and Constanstine, who died in A. D. 337, erected the church of St. John, without the walls of Rome, which, in fact, in its composition, resembles a Norman building, and it is curious to observe that the ornament afterwards used so profusely in Norman work, is used in the buildings of Dioclesian, whose Corinthian modillions are capped with a moulding cut in zigzag, and which only wants the enlargement of the moulding to become a real Norman ornament. When the Romans left the Island, it was most likely that the attempts of the Britons were still more rude, and endeavouring to imitate, but not executing on principle, the Roman work, their architecture became debased into the Saxon and early Norman, intermixed with ornaments perhaps brought in by the Danes. After the conquest, the rich Norman barons, erecting very magnificent castles and churches, the execution manifestly improved, though still with much similarity to the Roman mode debased; but the introduction of shafts, instead of the massive pier, first

began to approach that lighter mode of building,
which, by the introduction of the pointed arch, and
by an increased delicacy of execution, and boldness
of composition, ripened, at the close of the twelfth century, into the simple, yet beautiful Early English style.
At the close of another century, this style, from the
alteration of its windows, by throwing them into large
ones, divided by mullions, introducing tracery in the
heads of windows, and the general use of flowered
ornaments, together with an important alteration in
the piers, became the Decorated English style, which
may be considered as the perfection of the English
mode. This was very difficult to execute, from its
requiring flowing lines where straight ones were more
easily combined; and at the close of the fourteenth
century, we find these flowing lines giving way to perpendicular and horizontal ones, the use of which
continued to increase, till the arches were almost lost
in a continued series of pannels, which, at length, in
one building — the chapel of Henry the VII — covered
completely both the outside and inside; and the eye,
fatigued by the constant repetition of small parts,
sought in vain for the bold grandeur of design which
had been so nobly conspicuous in the preceding style.
The reformation, occasioning the destruction of many
of the buildings the most celebrated, and mutilating
others, or abstracting the funds necessary for their
repair, seems to have put an end to the working of the
English styles on principle; the square pannelled and
mullioned windows, with the wooden pannelled roofs
and halls, of the great houses of the time of Queen Elizabeth, seem rather a debased English than any thing
else; but during the reign of her successor, the Italian
architecture began to be introduced, first only in
columns of doors, and other small parts, and afterwards in larger portions, though still the general style
was this debased English. Of this introduction, the
most memorable is the celebrated tower of the schools
at Oxford, where, into a building adorned with pin-

nacles, and having mullioned windows, the architect has crowded all the five orders over each other. Some of the works of Inigo Jones are little removed beyond this barbarism. Longleat, in Wiltshire, is rather more advanced, and the banqueting-house, Whitehall, seems to mark the complete introduction of Roman workmanship. The close of the seventeenth century produced Sir Christopher Wren, a man whose powers, confessedly great, lead us to regret he had not studied the architecture of his English ancestors with the success he did that of Rome; for while he has raised the most magnificent modern building we possess, he seems to have been pleased to disfigure the English edifice he had to complete. His works at St. Mary Aldermary, and St. Dunstan in the east, prove how well he could execute imitated English buildings when he chose, though even in them he has departed, in several respects, from the true English principles. By the end of the seventeenth century, the Roman architecture appears to have been well established, and the works of Vitruvius and Palladio successfully studied; but Sir John Vanbrugh and Nicholas Hawksmoor seem to have endeavoured to introduce a massiveness of style which happily is peculiar to themselves. The works of Palladio, as illustrated by some carpenters, appear to have been the model for working the orders during the greatest part of the eighteenth century; but in the early and middle part of it, a style of ornament borrowed from the French was much introduced in interiors, the principal distinctions of which were the absence of all straight lines, and almost of all regular lines. The examples of this are now nearly extinct, and seem to have been driven out by the natural operation of the advance of good workmanship in the lower class of buildings.

All ornamental carvings were with difficulty executed in wood, and were very expensive; but towards the latter end of the eighteenth century, the Adams introduced a style of ornament directly contrary to the heavy carving of their predecessors. This was so flat as to be easily worked in plaster and other compositions, and ornament was sold very cheap, and profusely used in carpenters' work. This flatness was more or less visible in many considerable buildings; but near the close of the century, the magnificent works of Stuart and Revet, and the Ionian antiquities of the Dilletante Society, began to excite the public attention, and in a few years a great alteration was visible; the massive Doric, and the beautiful plain Grecian Ionic began to be worked, and our ordinary door-cases, &c. soon began to take a better character. The use of the simple, yet bold mouldings and ornaments of the Grecian models, is gradually spreading, and perhaps we may hope, from the present general investigation of the principles of science, that this will continue without danger of future debasement, and that a day may come when we shall have Grecian, Roman and English edifices erected on the principles of each.

GRECIAN ARCHITECTURE.

THE many valuable treatises and excellent delineations of the Grecian and Roman buildings, and the details of their parts, will render unnecessary, in this dissertation, that minuteness which, from the total absence of a previous system, it will be proper to adopt in the description of the English styles. But in this sketch a similar plan will be followed, of first giving the name and grand distinctions of the orders, then describing the terms and names of parts necessary for those who have not paid attention to the subject to understand, and a concise description of each order will follow; with respect to the examples in England, it will be most proper to leave the reader to select his own, because in this country we have not, as in the English architecture, the originals to study, but a variety of copies, adapted to the climate, and to the convenience of modern times.

In dividing the Grecian and Roman architecture, the word *order* is used, and much more properly than *style;* the English styles regard not a few parts, but the composition of the whole building, but a Grecian building is denominated Doric or Ionic, merely from its ornaments ; and the number of columns, windows, &c. may be the same in any order, only varied in their proportion.

The orders are generally considered to be five, and are usually enumerated as follows:

Tuscan,
Doric,
Ionic,
Corinthian,
Composite.

Their origin will be treated of hereafter. Their prominent distinctions are as follow:

The *Tuscan* is without any ornament whatever.

The *Doric* is distinguished by the channels and projecting intervals in the frieze, called *triglyphs*.

The *Ionic* by the ornaments of its capital, which are spiral, and are called *volutes*.

The *Corinthian* by the superior height of its capital, and its being ornamented with leaves, which support very small volutes.

The *Composite* has also a tall capital with leaves, but is distinguished from the Corinthian by having the large volutes and enriched ovolo of the Ionic capital.

In a complete order there are three grand divisions, which are occasionally executed separately, viz.

The *column*, including its base and capital,

The *pedestal*, which supports the column,

The *entablature*, or part above and supported by the column.

These are again each subdivided into three parts:

The *pedestal* into *base*, or lower mouldings ; *dado* or *die*, the plain central space; and *surbase*, or upper mouldings.

The *column* into *base*, or lower mouldings; *shaft*, or central space; and *capital*, or upper mouldings.

The *entablature*, into *architrave*, or part immediately above the column; *frieze*, or central flat space; and *cornice*, or upper projecting mouldings.

These parts may be again divided thus: the lower portions, viz. the base of the pedestal, base of the column, and the architrave, divide each into two parts; the first and second into plinth and mouldings, the third into face or faces, and upper moulding or tenia.

Each *central* portion, as dado of the pedestal, shaft of the column, and frieze, is undivided.

Each *upper* portion, as surbase of the pedestal, capital of the column, cornice of the entablature, divides into three parts: the first into *bedmould*, or the part under the corona; *corona*, or plain face; and *cymatium*, or upper moulding.

The *capital* into *neck*, or part below the ovolo;

ovolo, or projecting round moulding; and *abacus* or *tile*, the flat upper moulding, mostly nearly square. These divisions of the capital, however, are less distinct than those of the other parts.

The *cornice* into *bedmould*, or part below the corona; *corona*, or flat projecting face; *cymatium*, or moulding above the corona.

Besides these general divisions, it will be proper to notice a few terms often made use of.

The ornamental moulding running round an arch, or round doors and windows, is called an *architrave*.

A horizontal moulding for an arch to spring from, is called an *impost*.

The stone at the top of an arch, which often projects, is called a *key-stone*.

The small brackets under the corona in the cornice, are called *mutules* or *modillions;* if they are square, or longer in front than in depth, they are called *mutules*, and are used in the Doric order. If they are less in front than their depth, they are called *modillions*, and in the Corinthian order have carved leaves spread under them.

A *truss* is a modillion enlarged, and placed flat against a wall, often used to support the cornice of doors and windows.

A *console* is an ornament like a truss carved on a key-stone.

Trusses, when used under modillions in the frieze, are called *cantalivers*.

The space under the corona of the cornice, is called a *soffit*, as is also the under side of an arch.

Dentils are ornaments used in the bedmould of cornices; they are parts of a small flat face, which is cut perpendicularly, and small intervals left between each.

A flat column is called a *pilaster;* and those which are used with columns, and have a different capital, are called *antæ*.

A small height of pannelling above the cornice, is called an *attic;* and in these pannels, and sometimes in other parts, are introduced small pillars, swelling towards the bottom, called *balustres*, and a series of them a *balustrade*.

The triangular portion over a series of columns is called a *pediment*, and the plain space bounded by the horizontal and sloping cornices, the *tympanum;* this is often ornamented with figures or other work in relief.

Pedestals and attics are far from settled as to their proportions, or the mode of their execution, depending almost entirely on circumstances connected with the particular design, rather than the order they are used with. However, for pedestals, about one-fifth of the whole height, including pedestal and entablature, is a good proportion, though it may be often necessary to to alter it from local circumstances. In general an order looks much better, executed without pedestals.

Columns are sometimes ornamented by channels, which are called *flutes*. These channels are sometimes partly filled by a lesser round moulding; this is called *cabling* the flutes.

If the joints of the masonry are channelled, the work is called *rustic*, which is often used as a basement for an order.

For the better understanding the description to be given of the orders, it will be proper first to notice the mouldings which, by different combinations, form their parts.

The most simple mouldings are,

1st, The *ovolo*, or quarter round.

2nd, The *cavetto*, or hollow.

3rd, The *torus*, or round.

From the composition of these are formed divers others, and from the arrangement of them, with plain flat spaces between, are formed cornices and other ornaments. A large flat space is called a *corona*, if in the cornice; a *face* or *fascia* in the architrave; and the *frieze* itself is only a flat space. A small flat face is called a *fillet*, and is interposed between mouldings to divide them.

A fillet is, in the bases of columns and some other parts, joined to a face, or to the column itself by a small hollow, then called *apophyges.*

The torus, when very small, becomes an *astragal,* which projects; or a *bead,* which does not project.

Compound mouldings are, the *cyma recta,* which has the hollow uppermost and projecting.

The *cyma reversa,* or *ogee,* which has the round uppermost and projecting.

The *scotia,* which is formed of two hollows, one over the other, and of different centres.

In the Roman works, the mouldings are generally worked of equal projection to the height, and not bolder than the above regular forms; but the Grecian mouldings are often bolder, and worked with a small return, technically called a *quirk,* and these are of various proportions.

The ogee and ovolo are most generally used with quirks.

Several beads placed together, or sunk in a flat face, are called *reedings.*

All these mouldings, except the fillet, may be occasionally carved, and they are then called *enriched mouldings.*

From these few simple forms, (by adding astragals and fillets, and combining differently ornamented mouldings, faces, and soffits,) are all the cornices, pannels, and other parts formed, and the modern compositions in joiners, plasterers, and masons' work, are very numerous, and too well known to need describing.

There are several terms applied to large buildings, which it is proper also to explain.

A series of columns of considerable length, is called a *colonnade.*

A series of columns at the end of a building, or projecting from the side of a building, is called a *portico.*

A portico is called *tetra style,* if of four columns; *hexa style,* if of six; *octo style,* if of eight.

13

Tuscan Order.

Though this is not, perhaps, the most ancient of the orders, yet, from its plainness and simplicity, it is usually first noticed. Its origin is evidently Italian, for the Grecian work, however plain, has still some of the distinctive marks of massive Doric, whilst the Tuscan always bears clear marks of its analogy to the Roman Doric.

The pedestal, when used, is very plain, but the column is more often set on a plain square block plinth, which suits the character of the order better than the higher pedestal. This block projects about half the height of the plinth of the base beyond its face.

The column, including the base and capital, is about seven diameters high. The column, in the Roman orders, is sometimes only diminished the upper two-thirds of its height. This diminution is bounded by a curved line, which is variously determined, but does not differ much from what an even spring would assume, if one part of it were bound, in the direction of the axis of the shaft, to the cylindrical third, and then, by pressure at the top only, brought to the diminishing point. The Grecian columns are mostly diminished from the bottom, and conically. The quantity of diminution varies from one-sixth to one-fourth of the diameter just above the base.

The Tuscan base is half a diameter in height, and consists of a plain torus with a fillet and apophyges, which last is part of the shaft, and not of the base, as indeed all apophygæ are considered to be; and also all the astragals underneath the capitals, as well as the upper fillet of the base in all the richer orders, and in masonry should be executed on the shaft stones.

The capital of the Tuscan order is (exclusive of the astragal) half a diameter in height, and consists of a neck on which is an ovolo and fillet, joined to the neck by an apophyges, and over the ovolo a square tile, which is ornamented by a projecting fillet.

The shaft is never fluted, but many architects have given to this order, and some have even added to the richer orders, large square blocks, as parts of the shaft, which are called rustications, and are sometimes roughened.

The Tuscan entablature should be quite plain, having neither mutules nor modillions. The architrave has one or sometimes two faces, and a fillet; the frieze quite plain, and the cornice consisting of a cyma recta for cymatium, and the corona with a fillet, and a small channel for drip in the soffit. The bedmould should consist of an ovolo fillet and cavetto.

This Tuscan is that of Palladio; some other Italian architects have varied in parts, and some have given a sort of block modillions like those used in Covent Garden church, but these are of wood, and ought not to be imitated in stone.

This order is little used, and will most likely, in future, be still less so, as the massive Grecian Doric is an order equally manageable, and far more elegant.

Having explained the parts of one order, it will be necessary to make a few remarks, which could not so well be previously introduced. If pilasters and columns are used together, and they are of the same character, and not antæ, the pilasters should be diminished like the columns; but where pilasters are used alone, they may be undiminished.

The fillet and moulding under the cymatium, which, in rich orders, is often an ogee, is part of the corona, and as such is continued over the corona in the horizontal line of pediments, where the cymatium is omitted; and is also continued with the corona in interior work, where the cymatium is often with propriety omitted.

In pediments, whose cornices contain mutules, modillions, or dentils, those in the raking cornice must be placed perpendicularly over those in the horizontal cornice, and their sides must be perpendicular, though their under parts have the rake of the cornice

Doric Order.

The ancient Grecian Doric appears to have been an
order of peculiar grandeur; simple and bold, its ornaments were the remains of parts of real utility, and
perhaps originally it was worked with no moulding but
the cymatium, to cover the ends of the tiles, its triglyphs
being the ends of the beams, and its mutules those of
the rafters.   In after times, its proportions were made
rather less massive, and its mouldings and ornaments,
though not numerous, were very beautiful.   The
Romans considerably altered this order, and by the
regulations they introduced, rendered it peculiarly
difficult to execute on large buildings.   As the examples of the two countries are very different, we shall
treat of them separately, and therefore first of the

GRECIAN DORIC.

The columns of this order were, in Greece, generally
placed on the floor, without pedestal and without
base ; the capital, which occupied a height of about
half a diameter, had no astragal, but a few plain fillets,
with channels between them, under the ovolo, and a
small channel below the fillets.   The ovolo is generally
flat, and of great projection, with a quirk or return.
On this was laid the abacus, which was only a plain
tile, without fillet or ornament.

In the division of the entablature, the architrave
and frieze have each more than a third in height, and
the cornice less.   The architrave has only a plain broad
fillet, under which are placed the drops or guttæ,
which appear to hang from the triglyphs.

The triglyph, in Greece, appears to have been generally placed at the angle, thus bringing the interior
edge of the triglyph nearly over the centre of the
angular column.   The metope, or space between the
triglyphs, was nearly the square of the height of the
frieze, and a mutule was placed not only over each

triglyph, but also over each metope. The cornice of this order, in Greece, consisted of a plain face, under the mutule, which was measured as part of the frieze, and then the mutule, which projected sloping forward under the corona, so that the bottom of the mutule in front was considerably lower than at the back. Over the corona was commonly a small ovolo and fillet, and then a larger ovolo and fillet for the cymatium; and below the corona a fillet about equal in height to the mutule.

The ornaments of this order, in Greece, were, 1st, the flutings of the column, which are peculiar to the order, and are twenty in number, shallow, and not with fillets between them, but sharp edges. These flutes are much less than a semi-circle, and should be elliptic.

2nd, At the corner, in the space formed in the soffit of the corona, by the interval between the two angular mutules, was sometimes placed a flower, and the cymatium of the cornice had often lions' heads, which appear to have been real spouts.

3rd, In addition to the drops under the triglyph, the mutules also had several rows of drops of the same shape and size.

This order appears in general to have been worked very massive; the best examples are from five to six diameters high, which is lower than the Italians usually worked the Tuscan; but this gave peculiar grandeur to the temples in which it is thus employed.

Our present authorities for the Grecian orders are scattered through a variety of very expensive works, and in them presented in very irregular succession, whether we regard their supposed dates, their purity, or their orders; and it would be a valuable present to the architectural student, if the good authorities of each order were collected, figured, and some account given of their variations. With respect to the Doric order, this has been ably done in a treatise by Edmund Aikin, from which we shall take the liberty of extracting a few remarks.

" On viewing and comparing the examples of the Doric order, the first emotion will probably be surprise, at beholding the different proportions, — a diversity so great, that scarcely any two instances appear which do not materially differ in the relative size of their parts, both in general and in detail, and presenting differences which cannot be reconciled upon any system of calculation, whether the diameter or the height of the column, or the general height of the order be taken as the element of proportion. At the same time, they all resemble one another in certain characteristic marks, which denote the order; the differences are not generic, but specific, and leave unimpaired, those plain and obvious marks, which enable us to circumscribe the genuine Doric order, within a simple and easy definition.

" Interesting would be the investigation, could we trace the history of the Doric order in its monuments, and mark what progressive improvements it may have received in the course of time; but of the monuments of antiquity few, comparatively, have survived the injuries of time, and the more speedy and effectual destruction of violence; and of these still fewer retain either inscriptions, or, in the records of history, the dates of their erection."

The examples of Grecian Doric, of which we have accounts and figures, that may be depended on, are:

The temple of Minerva at Athens, called the Parthenon.

The temple of Theseus, at Athens.

The Propylea, at Athens.

The temple of Minerva, at Sunium.

The portico of the Agora, at Athens.

A temple at Corinth.

The temple of Jupiter Nemæus, between Argos and Corinth.

The temple of Apollo, at Delos.

The portico of Philip, at Delos.

The temple of Jupiter Pannellenius, in Ægina.

The temple of Minerva, at Syracuse.
The temple of Juno Lucina, at Agrigentum.
The temple of Concord, at Agrigentum.
The temple of Jupiter, at Selinus.
A smaller temple, at Selinus.
A temple at Ægesta.
Three temples at Pœstum.

Our limits will not permit us to enter minutely into the question, which of these examples might be now considered as the most valuable for imitation; but one circumstance it is requisite to notice, which is, that in the Athenian examples, and many of the others, the architrave projects over the top of the shaft, so as to be nearly perpendicular to the front of the bottom of the shaft, an arrangement never seen at Rome, but which contributes much to the boldness of the Grecian temples : and it is curious to observe, that in the temple of Apollo at Delos, of Concord at Agrigentum, and the temple at Ægesta, this projection is very small, compared with that of the other examples; and that in the portico of Philip, at Delos, and all the temples at Pœstum, there is no projection, but the face of the architrave is set over the diminished part of the shaft, the same as in Roman examples.

Two of the temples at Pœstum have capitals, with some trivial additions about the neck, and such a great projection of the echinus and abacus, as well as some appearances in the entablature, that take very much from their beauty.

The other temple at Pœstum has (excepting the projection above spoken of) all the characters of the Grecian examples.

On the whole, the temples of Minerva and Theseus at Athens, and Minerva at Sunium, appear those examples which deserve the most attentive consideration, as well from the general beauty of the composition, as the excellence of the details and execution. But in this order, as well as in Architecture generally, the duty of the Architect is not to be a servile copyist of any example, however fine, but by seizing the principles and spirit, of the age of his best models, to form such a composition as, by its fitness for the purpose to which it is applied, should appear that edifice which, for a similar purpose, the great Architects, whose works he seeks rather to renew than imitate, would have erected.

ROMAN DORIC.

This differs from the Grecian in several important particulars, which will appear from the following rules: from the strictness of which follows that extreme difficulty of execution which has been so often complained of in this order: 1st, the triglyphs must be precisely over the centre of the columns; 2d, the metopes must be exact squares; 3d, the mutules also must be exact squares.

As, therefore, the intercolumniation must be of a certain number of triglyphs, it will be easily conceived how difficult it will be, in large buildings, where a triglyph is several feet, to accommodate this order to the internal arrangements.

The Roman Doric is sometimes set on a plinth, and sometimes on a pedestal, which should be of few and plain mouldings. The bases usually employed, are either the attic base of a plinth, lower torus, scotia, and upper torus, with fillets between them, or the proper base of one torus and an astragal; or, in some instances, of a plinth, and simple fillet. The shaft, including the base and capital, each of which is half a diameter, is generally eight diameters high, and is fluted like the Grecian. The capital has an astragal and neck under the ovolo, which has sometimes three small fillets projecting over each other, and sometimes another astragal and fillet. The ovolo should be a true quarter round. The abacus has a small ogee and fillet on its upper edge.

The architrave has less height than the Grecian, being only two-thirds of the frieze, which is equal in height to the cornice. In a few instances the architrave has two faces, but mostly only one.

The frieze has nothing peculiar to this mode; if plain, its metopes being, as before observed, square.

The cornice differs much from the Grecian, having its soffit flat, and the mutules square, with a square interval between them. The Grecian drops in the mutules generally appear in front, below the mutules; but the Roman do not, and are sometimes omitted; the drops also are of a different shape, being more complete cones.

The cymatium is often a cavetto, and sometimes a cyma recta, with an ogee under it. The mutules have a small ogee, which runs round them, and also round the face they are formed of; and under the mutules are an ovolo and small fillet, and the flat fillet which runs round the top of the triglyphs here belongs to the cornice, and not, as in the Grecian, to the frieze.

The Roman Doric is susceptible of much ornament, for in addition to the flutes, the guttæ of the triglyphs, and the roses in the soffit of the corona, the neck of the capital has sometimes eight flowers or husks placed round it, the ovolo carved, and the metopes in the frieze filled with alternate ox-skulls and pateræ, or other ornaments. In interior decorations, sometimes one or two of the mouldings of the cornice are enriched; but with all this ornament, the Roman Doric is far inferior, in real beauty, to the Grecian.

The Doric we have now described, and its rules, should rather be considered Italian than Roman; for it is in fact the Doric worked by modern Italian architects, rather than the Doric of ancient Rome, of which we have only one example, which is far from giving such a Doric as above described.

This example is the theatre of Marcellus, which has dentils in the cornice, and of which the corona

was so decayed even near 150 years back, as to give
no trace of any thing but an indication of a mutule,
which appears a little like a Grecian mutule. This
theatre is considered to have been erected by Augustus,
and it appears most probable that the portico of the
Agora, at Athens, was erected about the same time;
if so, it becomes a curious question, how and why the
order should be so altered in Rome.

The first order of the Coliseum is a much later
work, and is extremely poor in its combinations, but
has a capital very much like the theatre of Marcellus,
and its cornice has an uncut dentil face.

Ionic Order.

As the Greeks and Romans differed much in their
modes of working the Doric Order, so there was
considerable difference in their execution of the Ionic,
though by no means so great as in the former.

The distinguishing feature of this order is the
capital, which has four spiral projections called volutes.
These in Greece were placed flat on the front and back
of the column, leaving the two sides of a different
character, and forming a balustre; but this at the
external angle producing a disagreeable effect, an
angular volute was sometimes placed there, showing
two volutes, one flat the other angular, to each
exterior face, and a balustre to each interior; but this
not forming a good combination, a capital was invented
with four angular volutes, and the abacus with its
sides hollowed out. This is called the *modern* Ionic
capital. In the *ancient*, the list or spiral line of the
volute runs along the face of the abacus, straight
under the ogee; but in the modern, this list springs
from behind the ovolo, and in the hollow of the abacus,
which is an ovolo, fillet, and cavetto, is generally
placed a flower. The abacus of the ancient capital
has only a small ogee for its moulding.

There are examples at Athens of an astragal to the
ancient Ionic capital below the volutes, leaving a neck

which is adorned with carvings, but these examples are rare.

The Ionic shaft, including the base, which is half a diameter, and the capital to the bottom of the volute generally a little more, is about nine diameters high.

The pedestal is a little taller, and more ornamented than the Doric.

The bases used to this order are very various; some of the Grecian examples are of one torus and two scotiæ, with astragals and fillets; others of two large tori and a scotia of small projection; but the attic base is very often used, and with an astragal added above the upper torus, makes a beautiful and appropriate base for the Ionic.

The cornices of this order may be divided into three divisions; 1st, the plain Grecian cornice; 2nd, the dentil cornice; 3d, the modillion cornice.

In the first, the architrave is of one or two faces; the frieze plain, and the cornice composed of a corona with a deep soffit, and the bedmould moulding hidden by the drip of the soffit, or coming very little below it. The cymatium generally a cyma recta, and ogee under it.

The second has generally two faces in the architrave, and the cornice, which is rather more than one-third of the height of the entablature, has a corona with a cyma recta and ogee for cymatium, and for bedmould a dentil face between an ovolo and ogee. The soffit of the corona is sometimes ornamented.

The third, or modillion entablature, has the same architrave, frieze, and cymatium of its cornice as the last, but under the soffit of the corona are placed modillions, which are plain, and surrounded by a small ogee; one must be placed over the centre of each column, and one being close to the return, makes a square pannel in the soffit at the corner, and between each modillion, which is often filled with a flower.

The bedmould below is generally an ovolo fillet and cavetto.

This modillion cornice is, in fact, as well as the capital, rather Italian than Roman, as the ancient examples have the dentil cornice; and in point of time, there may be some doubt, whether the modern Ionic capital is not rather a deduction from the Composite than the contrary; for the angular volute of Greece is not such a one as, if repeated, would make the modern Ionic capital. The alteration of this order is in many respects valuable, for although not equal in simplicity to the Grecian Ionic, yet it is so easily manageable, especially with a dentil cornice, as to be easily adapted to modern wants; and when executed on a large scale, the modillion cornice has a bold effect. The great difficulty in the Grecian Ionic is the return at the angle; it does not look well to have a column sideways in a range with others fronting, and this arrangement is so often wanted, and so ill attained by the Greek angular volute, that many times there is no alternative but the use of the modern capital.

It was once the custom to work the Ionic frieze projecting like a torus, thus giving an awkward weight to an order which ought to be light. The introduction of good Grecian models has driven out this impropriety, and much improved the present execution of the order, which is very beautiful, if well executed.

The Ionic shaft may be fluted in twenty-four flutes, with fillets between them; these flutes are semi-circular. This order may be much ornamented if necessary, by carving the ovolo of the capital, the ogee of the abacus, and one or two mouldings of both architrave and cornice; but the ancient Ionic looks extremely well without any ornament whatever.

Our Ionic examples are not so numerous as the Doric, nor so complete, several of them not being entirely figured without conjecture. They are:

The temple on the Illisus, at Athens.

The temples in the Acropolis, of Minerva Polias, and Erichtheus.

The aqueduct of Adrian, at Athens.

The temple of Apollo Didymeus, at Miletus.

The temple of Bacchus, at Teos.

The temple of Minerva Polias, at Priene.

The temple of Fortuna Virilis, at Rome.

Of these, for simplicity and elegance of composition, the now-destroyed temple on the Illissus, is pre-eminent; its volutes plain, but of excellent proportion, and it had an angular volute to the external capital; its base was in mouldings the attic, but the tori were large, and the scotia flat; there was a small astragal above the upper torus, and that torus was cut into small flutes. The entablature was very plain, having an architrave of one face only, a frieze plain, but which there is some reason to suppose was carved in some parts, and a corona with deep soffit, and for bedmould only an ogee, with a fillet above, and astragal below.

The temples in the Acropolis are small, but extremely rich, having many members carved. The cornice is the same as the last example, but the architrave is of three faces. There are three ranges of columns, and the capitals of each have minute differences, but they may all be described together: they have an ornamented neck and astragal below the volutes; the fillets of the volutes are double, thus making the volute much more elaborate, though not more beautiful; the bases are enriched with carvings, and the columns fluted; the bases are nearly those of the last example, but want the astragal. Of these examples, the architraves have a small projection from the top of the column, though not near so much as the Doric.

The aqueduct of Adrian is plain, but of good composition; it has a good volute, an architrave of two faces, and a small projection in front of the column; a plain frieze, and a good plain dentil cornice.

The temples of Minerva Polias, at Priene, and Apollo, at Miletus, have a base which is curious, but by no means deserving of imitation; it consists of a large torus, resting on two scotiæ, which are divided from it, and from each other and the plinth, by two astragals at each division. This base gives the column so unsteady an appearance, that it spoils an otherwise beautiful order.

The temple of Bacchus, at Teos, has an attic base with an astragal added, and a cornice with dentils of of greater projection than usual. These three last examples have their volutes smaller than those of Athens, which takes much from the grandeur of the order.

The temple of Fortuna Virilis, at Rome. This example is far inferior to those we have before noticed. The Romans seem to have had a singular predilection, particularly in their declining works, for very large fillets, and it is abundantly shown in this edifice, where the fillet of the tenia of the architrave is very nearly as large as the ogee under it, and larger than one face of the architrave; this, though the capital is pretty good, spoils the order, and the cornice is poor from the trifling appearance of the corona. The base is the attic of very good proportion.

The temple of Concord, at Rome, is figured by *Desgodets*, but it is only remarkable for its deformity, and having an appearance of the modern Ionic. The capitals have angular volutes, but under the usual ovolo and astragal is a cyma recta, enriched with leaves, and a large astragal and fillet. The entablature is of a very poor character, and has small dentils and large plain modillions. The base is of two tori divided by two scotiæ, which are separated by a fillet. In this example, the fillet on the bottom of the shaft is nearly as large as the upper torus.

Corinthian Order.

This order originated in Greece, and the capital is
said to have been suggested by observing a tile placed
on a basket left in a garden, and round which sprung
up an acanthus. All the other orders have, in various
countries and situations, much variety; but the
Corinthian, though not without slight variations, even
in the antique, is much more settled in its proportions,
and its greater or less enrichment is the principal
source of variety.

The capital is the great distinction of this order; its
height is more than a diameter, and consists of an
astragal, fillet and apophyges, all of which are measured
with the shaft, then a bell and horned abacus. The
bell is set round with two rows of leaves, eight in each
row, and a third row of leaves supports eight small
open volutes, four of which are under the four horns
of the abacus, and the other four, which are sometimes
interwoven, are under the central recessed part of
the abacus, and have over them a flower or other
ornament. These volutes spring out of small twisted
husks placed between the leaves of the second row,
and which are called *caulicoles*. The abacus consists
of an ovolo, fillet, and cavetto, like the modern Ionic.
There are various modes of indenting the leaves,
which are called, from these variations, *acanthus*,
olive, &c. The column, including the base of half a
diameter, and the capital, is about ten diameters high.

Of the Corinthian capital, although the best examples have all some trifling difference, principally in the
raffling of the leaves, and the connexion of the central
small volutes; yet there is one capital so different from
the others that it deserves some remark, more especially
as it has been lately introduced into some considerable
edifices. This capital is that of the circular temple
at Tivoli, called by some a temple of Vesta, by others
the Sybils' temple. In this capital the angular
volutes are large, so much so as to give the capital the

air of a Composite, till more minutely examined; it is
however a real Corinthian, for it has central volutes,
though they are small, and formed out of the stalks
themselves, and not as in the ordinary capital rising
from them. Its great beauty, however, is the very
bold manner of raffling the leaves, which gives it a
very different appearance from the other capitals, and
one which, in particular circumstances, may make it
valuable. The flower over the centre volutes, is
very different from the common one, and much larger.

If a pedestal is used, it should have several mouldings, some of which may, if necessary, be enriched.
The base may be either an attic base, or with the
addition of three astragals, one over each torus, and
one between the scotia and upper torus; or a base of
two tori and two scotiæ, which are divided by two
astragals, and this seems the most used to the best
examples; one or two other varieties sometimes occur.

The entablature of this order is very fine. The
architrave has mostly two or three faces, which have
generally small ogees or beads between them,

The frieze is flat, but is often joined to the upper
fillet of the architrave by an apophyges

The cornice has both modillions and dentils, and is
usually thus composed; above the corona is a cymatium, and small ogee; under it the modillions, whose
disposition, like the Ionic, must be one over the
centre of the column, and one close to the return of
the cornice.

These modillions are carved with a small balustre
front, and a leaf under them; they are surrounded at
the upper part by a small ogee and fillet, which also
runs round the face they spring from. Under the
modillions is placed an ovolo, and then a fillet and the
dentil face, which is often left uncut in exterior work.
Under the dentils are a fillet and ogee. In some cases
this order is properly worked with a plain cornice,
omitting the modillions, and leaving the dentil face
uncut.

The enrichments of this order may be very considerable; some of the mouldings of the pedestal and base may be enriched; the shaft may be fluted, as the Ionic, in twenty-four flutes, which may be filled one-third high by staves, which is called *cabling* the flutes; the small mouldings of the architrave, and even some of its faces, and several mouldings of the cornice, may be enriched; the squares in the soffit of the corona pannelled and flowered, and the frieze may be adorned with carvings. But though the order will bear all this ornament without overloading it, yet, for exteriors, it seldom looks better than when the capitals and the modillions are the only carvings.

The principal Corinthian examples are in Rome; there are, however, some Grecian examples, which we shall first notice:

A portico, at Athens.

The arch of Adrian, at Athens.

The Incantada, at Salonica.

A temple at Jackly, near Mylassa.

Of these, the first has an entablature, which is almost exactly that which has been generally used for the Composite; the others have all dentil cornices, without modillions. In two examples, the horns of the abacus, instead of being cut off as usual, are continued to a point, which gives an appearance of weakness to the capital. The bases are mostly attic, with an additional astragal, and at Jackly the tori are carved.

The temple of Vesta, at Tivoli, has the capital noticed above; its entablature is simple, with an uncut dentil face, and the frieze carved in festoons. The astragal, under the capital, has a fillet above, as well as below, and the base has a fillet under the upper torus omitted. The flutes are stopt square, and not as usual rounded at the ends.

The remain, called the frontispiece of Nero, has the complete block entablature, usually called Composite. The capitals good, with attic base, and the whole of good character.

The temple of Vesta, at Rome,
The Basilica of Antoninus, and
The temple of Mars the Avenger,
are all incomplete; the first has pointed horns, and
the two first the attic base.

The temple of Antoninus and Faustina, and
The portico of Severus,
have both a cornice with dentil face only, and uncut;
the first an attic base.

The baths of Dioclesian have a good entablature, and
the attic base; some of the capitals are Composite.

The forum of Nerva,
The inner order of the Pantheon,
The outer order of the Pantheon,
The temple called Jupiter Tonans, and
The temple called Jupiter Stator,
are all excellent, and beautiful in their proportions and
execution; the fillets small, and the order much
enriched. The forum of Nerva, and the temple of
Jupiter Tonans, have no bases visible; the others have
the real Corinthian base with two scotiæ. The last may
be considered the best existing model of Corinthian;
it is one of the most enriched, and nothing can better
stamp its value than a minute and rigorous examination of it with any of the other examples.

These are only a part of the antique remains of this
order, but they are the best known, and may be
sufficient to induce the student to examine every
example for himself.

It will not be right to quit this order without
adverting to two stupendous magazines of it, the ruins
of Balbec and Palmyra; but although they are worth
examining as matters of curiosity, they are of comparatively little value; however rich, they contain
much of the faulty and crowded detail of the later
Roman work, and to what extent this was carried in
very great Roman works, the best evidence is the
palace of Dioclesian, at Spalatro, where, amidst a
profusion of ornament, we meet with great poverty

of composition, and combinations of mouldings so barbarous as to lead to a degree of astonishment, how they could be executed by persons before whose eyes were existing such examples as Rome even now contains. In the decline of the Roman empire, it became a fashion to remove columns; there are therefore in Rome, many edifices with a variety of valuable columns erected without their own entablature; and Constantine, in the church of St. Paul without the walls, began the Norman arrangement by springing arches off the columns without an entablature, and carrying up the wall to the clerestory windows, with little or no projection; thus annihilating the leading feature of the orders—a bold cornice.

Composite Order.

The Romans are said to have formed this order by mixing the Corinthian and Ionic capitals; like the Corinthian, the capital is its principal distinction. This is of the same height as the Corinthian, and it is formed by setting, on the two lower rows of the leaves of the Corinthian capital, the modern Ionic volutes, ovolo, and abacus. The small space left of the bell is filled by caulicoles, with flowers, and the upper list of the volute is often flowered.

From the great variety of capitals which are not Corinthian, (for it seems most commodious to term those only Corinthian which have four volutes in each face, or rather eight sets round the capital; four at the angles and four in the centre,) it may seem at first difficult to say what should be called *Composite*, and what considered as merely a *Composed order;* but there appears an easy way of designating the real Composite capital, viz. that of considering the Ionic volute, and the Ionic ovolo and astragal under the abacus, as essential parts; for this ovolo and astragal not existing in Corinthian capitals, forms a regular distinction between the two.

The column is of the same height as the Corinthian, and the pedestal and base differ very little from those of that order, the pedestal being sometimes a little plainer, and the base having an astragal or two less.

The entablature mostly used with this order is plainer than the Corinthian, having commonly only two faces to the architrave, the upper mouldings being rather bolder; and the cornice is different, in having, instead of the modillion and dentil, a sort of plain double modillion, consisting of two faces, the upper projecting farthest, and separated from the lower by a small ogee; under this modillion is commonly a large ogee, astragal, and fillet. The assumption of this entablature for the Composite is rather Italian than Roman, for the examples of Composite capitals in Rome have other entablatures, and this is found with Corinthian capitals; but we must suppose that Palladio and Scammozzi, who both give this cornice to the Composite, had some authority on which they acted, and considering the great destruction of ancient buildings for their columns, this is not improbable.

A plain cornice, nearly like that used to the Corinthian order, is sometimes used to this order, and also a cornice with the modillions bolder, and cantalivers under them in the frieze.

This order may be enriched in the same manner as the Corinthian.

The Composite examples we have to notice are few, and these are,

The temple of Bacchus,

The arch of Septimus Severus, and

The arch of the Goldsmiths.

These are all at Rome, and all have an attic base; they have all large fillets. The first entablature is plain, and has no dentil face; the second has a dentil face cut, as has the third, but the latter has an awkward addition of a second ogee under the dentils, apparently taken out of the frieze, which is thus made very small.

The baths of Dioclesian:—this example is placed in the same room with Corinthian columns; it has an attic base, and the Corinthian entablature.

The arch of Titus:—this example has a real Corinthian base and entablature; in short, it has nothing Composite but the capital.

On the whole, an attentive examination of the subject will lead us rather to discourage the use of this order than otherwise; it cannot be made so elegant an order as the Corinthian, and can only be wanted when columns are to be in two ranges; and then the capital of the temple of Vesta, at Tivoli, affords a sufficient alteration of the Corinthian.

Having gone through the forms and distinctions of the orders, it is proper to say, that, even in Greece and Rome, we meet with specimens whose proportions and composition do not agree with any of them. These are comprised under the general name of *Composed orders*, and though some are beautiful as small works, scarcely any of the ancient ones are worthy of imitation in large buildings. Of these composed orders we have two examples in the Pantheon, one in the columns of an altar, and the other in the pilasters of the attic: they have both dentil cornices, with an uncut face; the first has angular Corinthian volutes, and none in the centres, and water leaves instead of raffled leaves under the volutes; the other has no real volutes, but a scroll-work gives the appearance of them, and this capital is only fitted for pilasters. Modern composition has run very wild, and produced scarcely any thing worth prolonging by description. There was, however, one attempt of a singular kind, made some years since by an architect at Windsor, who published a magnificent treatise, and executed one colonnade and a few door-cases in and near Windsor. This was H. Emlyn, who conducted the restoration of St. George's chapel. His order, he says, was first brought into his mind by the twin trees in Windsor forest. He makes an oval shaft rise about one-fourth of its height, and then two round shafts spring from it, close to each other, and the diminution affords space for two capitals, which have volutes, and instead of leaves, feathers like the caps of the knights of the garter. His entablature has triglyphs, and his cornice mutules. The triglyphs are ostrich feathers, the guttæ acorns, and the metopes are filled with the star of the garter.

To conceal the awkward junction of the two columns to the lower part, an ornament is placed there, which is a trophy with the star of the garter in the centre.

It is obvious that this order must be extremely unmanageable, as it is difficult, and indeed almost impossible to make a good angle column, and if its entablature is proportioned to the diameter of one column, it will be too small; if to the whole diameter it will be too heavy, and a mean will give the capitals wrong; so that in any shape some error arises. In the colonnade above mentioned, the entablature is so light as to appear preposterous. This attempt is not generally known, as the book was very expensive, and the colonnade at a distance from a public road; but it deserves consideration, because, though the idea was new, its execution seems completely to have failed, and indeed in large designs, no composed order has ever yet appeared that can come into competition with a scrupulous attention to those excellent models of Greece and Rome, now, through the effects of graphic art, happily so familar to almost every English architect.

There are a few small buildings in and near Athens, which, though not coming within any of the orders precisely, are yet so beautiful in some of their parts, as to require express notice. These are,

The Choragic monument of Thrasyllus,

The octagon tower of Andronicus Cyrrhestes, called the temple of the Winds,

The Choragic monument of Lysicrates, called the lantern of Demosthenes, and

The temple of Pandrosus.

The first is now merely a face, its intervals being walled up, but was originally the front of a cavern, and consists of an entablature supported by three antæ, and covered by an attic lowered in the middle, on which is a statue in a sitting posture. The mouldings of the antæ are such as are used in Doric buildings, and the architrave is capped by a plain fillet, with a small fillet, and guttæ below; the guttæ are continued along with an interval about equal to each drop. The frieze contains eleven wreaths of laurel, and the cornice and attic mouldings are plain but very good.

The whole of this monument is so simple, yet possesses so beautiful a character as to render it worthy of very attentive study.

The temple of the Winds is chiefly valuable for its sculpture; it had two door-ways of a composed order, and in the interior is a small order of a Doric, of very inferior proportions, which rises to the support of the roof from a plain string, below which are two cornices or rather tablets. The roof is of marble cut into the appearance of tiles. The outside walls are plain, with an entablature, and a string below, forming a sort of frieze, on which are the figures of the winds. On the whole, this monument is rather curious than beautiful.

The lantern of Demosthenes. This is one of the most beautiful little remains of antiquity existing. The whole height is but thirty-four feet, and its diameter eight feet. It is a circular temple, with six engaged columns standing on a basement, nearly as high as the columns, and nearly solid. The capitals, though not like most Corinthian capitals, are very beautiful. The frieze is sculptured, and instead of a cymatium to the cornice, is an ornament of honey-suckles, and above that on the roof, which is beautifully carved in leaves, is a line of a waved projecting ornament; on the top is a vase, or rather the base of a tripod. Our limits will not admit of particularizing all the singularities of this delicate building, but it well deserves study and imitation.

The temple of Pandrosus is a building with Cary-atidæ, or figures instead of columns; they have each a capital of an ornamented square abacus, and ovolo carved. The entablature has no frieze, but an archi-trave of three faces, the uppermost of which has plain circles for ornament, and joins the cornice, which is a dentil cornice, large, and of good mouldings. The statues are good, and stand upon a continued pedestal of two-thirds their own height; and there are two antæ which descend through the pedestal, and the entablature is rather proportioned to these antæ than the Caryatidæ. Many of the mouldings are enriched, and indeed the whole of this curious building, which comprises the temples of Eryctheus, Minerva Polias, and Pandrosus, is a fruitful source of most delicate enrichment.

In this essay it has by no means been intended to mention every valuable remaining example; all that has been aimed at, is to give a general view of those remains which must be considered as standards, and to excite in the pupil that persevering attention to the best models, which is the only way of arriving at a complete knowledge of these very interesting sources of architectural science.

Description of the Plates of Grecian Architecture.

PLATE I.

The Tuscan order without a pedestal, having all its parts, and their members divided, with the names attached.

The various kinds of what are usually considered simple mouldings, with their names, and a portion of an arch with an architrave springing from an impost.

PLATE II.

Outlines of the Grecian and Roman Doric. The Grecian nearly accords with the best Athenian examples, but on this scale the minute parts cannot be shown of their exact size, particularly the fillets of the capital. The Roman is that which has been many years used in England, as the standard of Roman Doric, and is nearly that of Palladio.

PLATE III.

The Grecian and Roman Ionic. The parts of the Grecian have been taken from various examples, in order to combine as much as possible in one the general appearance of the order. The Roman is the modern Ionic of the Italian architects, as it has been executed for many years in England with the modillion cornice. The attic base has been applied in both instances, from the difficulty of executing a more complicated one distinctly on so small a scale; and when once this base is clearly comprehended, any other will be easily understood by the description in the former part of this work.

PLATE IV.

The Corinthian and Composite orders. The Corinthian capital is the one most commonly used, and is nearly that of the temple of Jupiter Tonans; the capital of the temple of Jupiter Stator is too much enriched, and the intersection of the middle volutes too delicate, to be shown on so small a scale; and for the same reason the attic base is used in this plate as well as the last.

The example given of the Composite order has been used in England for many years; and the entablature is that which appears most suited to the order.

PLATE I.

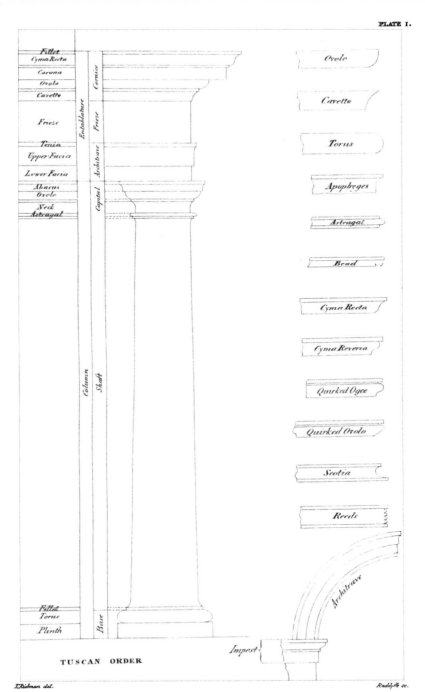

Fillet
Cyma Recta
Corona
Ovolo
Cavetto

Freze

Tenia
Upper Facia
Lower Facia
Abacus
Ovolo
Neck
Astragal

Cornice

Freze

Architrave

Capital

Entablature

Column

Shaft

Fillet
Torus
Plinth

Base

TUSCAN ORDER

Ovolo

Cavetto

Torus

Apophyges

Astragal

Bead

Cyma Recta

Cyma Reversa

Quirked Ogee

Quirked Ovolo

Scotia

Reeds

Architrave

Impost

T. Rickman del.

Radclyffe sc.

Published by J & J. Smith, Liverpool, 1 July, 1817.

Printed by W & T. Radclyffe.

PLATE II.

GRECIAN DORIC   ROMAN DORIC

T.Rickman del.   Radclyffe sc.

Published by J&J.Smith.Liverpool. 1.July. 1817.
Printed by W & E.Radclyffe.

PLATE III.

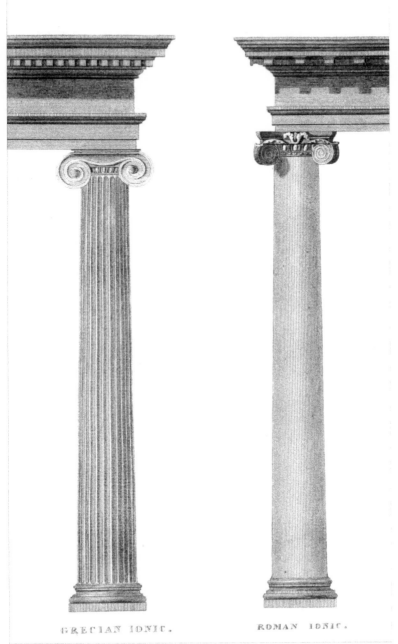

GRECIAN IONIC.   ROMAN IONIC.

T. Rickman del.   W. Radclyffe sc.

Published by J & J. Smith, Liverpool, 1 July, 1817.

Printed by W & T. Radclyffe.

PLATE IV.

CORINTHIAN.

COMPOSITE.

T. Rickman del.

W. Radclyffe sc.

Published by I & I. Smith. Liverpool. 1 July 1817

Printed by W & I. Radclyffe.

ENGLISH ARCHITECTURE.

IN a work like the present, there will be little
propriety in a lengthened disquisition on the origin of
this mode of building; we shall therefore proceed to
the detail of those distinctions, which, being once laid
down with precision, will enable persons of common
observation to distinguish the difference of age and
style in these buildings, as easily as the distinctions of
the Grecian and Roman orders.

It may, however, be proper here to offer a few
remarks on the use of the term English, as applied to
that mode of building usually called the Gothic, and
by some the pointed architecture. Although, perhaps,
it might not be so difficult as it has been supposed to
be, to show that the English architects were, in many
instances, prior to their continental neighbours, in
those advances of the styles about which so much has
been written, and so little concluded; it is not on
that ground the term is now used, but because, as far
as the author has been able to collect from plates, and
many friends who have visited the Continent, in the
edifices there, (more especially in those parts which
have not been at any time under the power of
England,) the architecture is of a very different character from that pure simplicity and boldness of
composition which marks the English buildings.
In every instance which has come under the author's
notice, a mixture, more or less exact or remote,
according to circumstances, of Italian composition, in
some parts or other, is present ; and he has little doubt
that a *very* attentive observation of the continental
buildings called Gothic, would enable an architect to
lay down the regulations of French, Flemish, Spanish,
German, and Italian styles, which were in use at the
time when the English flourished in England.

On the origin of the pointed arch, about which,
perhaps, there may be now more curiosity than ever,

from the numerous accounts given by travellers of apparently very ancient pointed arches in Asia, Africa, and various parts of the Continent; it will, doubtless, be expected that something should be said; and what is necessary may be said in a few lines. To say nothing on the impossibility, as far as at present appears, of fixing an *authentic* date to those, which if dated, might be of the most importance, there appears little difficulty in solving the problem, if the practical part of building is considered at the same time with the theoretical. Intersecting arches were most likely an early, and certainly a very widely-spread mode of embellishing Norman buildings, and some of them were constructed in places, and with stones, requiring centres to turn them on, and the construction of these centres must have been by something equivalent to compasses: thus, even supposing (which could hardly have been the case) that the arches were constructed without a previous delineation, the centres would have led to the construction of the pointed arch; and when once formed, its superior lightness and applicability would be easily observed. To this remark it may be added, that the arches necessarily arising in some parts from Norman groining would be pointed.— A careful examination of a great number of Norman buildings will also lead to this conclusion—that the style was constantly assuming a lighter character, and that the gradation is so gentle into Early English, that it is difficult, in some buildings, to class them, so much have they of both styles: the same may be said of every advance; and this seems to be a convincing proof that the styles were the product of the gradual operations of a general improvement, guided by the hand of genius, and not a foreign importation.

During the eighteenth century, various attempts, under the name of Gothic, have arisen in repairs and rebuilding ecclesiastical edifices, but these have been little more than making clustered columns and pointed windows, every real principle of English architecture being, by the builders, either unknown or totally neglected.

English architecture, may be divided into four distinct periods, or styles, which may be named,

1st, the Norman style,

2nd, the Early English style,

3rd, the Decorated English style, and

4th, the Perpendicular English style.

The dates of these styles we shall state hereafter, and it may be proper to notice, that the clear distinctions are now almost entirely confined to churches; for the destruction and alteration of castellated buildings have been so great, from the changes in the modes of warfare, &c. that, in them, we can scarcely determine what is original and what addition.

Before we treat of the styles separately, it will be necessary to explain a few terms which are employed in describing the churches and other buildings which exemplify them,

Most of the ancient ecclesiastical edifices, when considered complete, were built in the form of a cross, with a tower, lantern, or spire erected at the intersection. The interior space was usually thus divided:

The space westward of the cross, is called the *nave*.

The divisions outward of the piers, are called *aisles*.

The space eastward of the cross, is generally the *choir*.

The part running north and south, is called the *cross* or *transept*.

The choir is generally enclosed by a *screen*, on the western part of which is usually placed the organ.

The choir, in cathedrals, does not generally extend to the eastern end of the building, but there is a space behind the altar, usually called the *lady chapel*.

The choir is only between the piers, and does not include the side aisles, which serve as passages to the lady chapel, altar, &c.

The transept has sometimes *side aisles*, which are often separated by screens for chapels.

Chapels are attached to all parts, and are frequently additions.

The aisles of the nave are mostly open to it, and in cathedrals both are generally without pews.

In churches not collegiate, the eastern space about the altar is called the *chancel*.

To the sides are often attached small buildings over the doors, called *porches*, which have sometimes vestries, schools, &c. over them.

The *font* is generally placed in the western part of the nave, but in small churches its situation is very various. In a few churches a building like a chapel has been erected over the font, or the font set in it.

In large churches, the great doors are generally either at the west end, or at the end of the transepts, or both; but in small churches, often at the sides.

To most cathedrals are attached a *chapter-house* and *cloisters*, which are usually on the same side.

The *chapter-house* is often multangular.

The *cloisters* are generally a quadrangle, with an open space in the centre; the side to which is a series of arches, originally often glazed, now mostly open. The other wall is generally one side of the church or other buildings, with which the cloisters communicate by various doors. The cloisters are usually arched over, and formed the principal communication between the different parts of the monastery, for most of the large cross churches have been monasteries.

The lady chapel is not always at the east end of the choir; at Durham it is at the west end of the nave, at Ely on the north side.

The choir sometimes advances westward of the cross, as at Westminster.

The spaces in the interior, between the arches, are *piers*.

Any building above the roof may be called a *steeple*. If it be square-topt, it is called a *tower*.

A tower may be round, square, or multangular. The tower is often crowned with a spire, and sometimes with a short tower of light work, which is called a *lantern*.   An opening into the tower, in the interior, above the roof, is also called a lantern.

Towers, of great height in proportion to their diameter, are called *turrets;* these often contain staircases, and are sometimes crowned with small spires.

Large towers have often turrets at their corners, and often one larger than the others, containing a staircase; sometimes they have only that one.

The projections at the corners, and between the windows, are called *buttresses*, and the mouldings and slopes which divide them into stages, are called *set-offs*.

The walls are crowned by a *parapet*, which is straight at the top, or a *battlement* which is indented; both may be plain, or sunk pannelled, or pierced.

In castellated work, the battlement sometimes projects, with intervals for the purpose of discharging missiles on the heads of assailants; these openings are called *machicolations*.

Arches are round, pointed, or mixed :

A *semi-circular arch* has its centre in the same line with its spring.

A *segmental arch* has its centre lower than the spring.

A *horse-shoe arch* has its centre above the spring.

Pointed arches are either *equilateral*—described from two centres, which are the whole breadth of the arch from each other, and form the arch about an equilateral triangle; or *drop arches*, which have a radius shorter than the breadth of the arch, and are described about an obtuse-angled triangle; or *lancet arches*, which have a radius longer than the breadth of the arch, and are described about an acute-angled triangle.

All these pointed arches may be of the nature of segmental arches, and have their centres below their spring.

Mixed arches are of three centres, which look nearly like elliptical arches; or of four centres, commonly called the *Tudor arch;* this is flat for its span, and has two of its centres in or near the spring, and the other two far below it.

The *ogee* or *contrasted arch* has four centres ; two in or near the spring, and two above it and reversed.

The spaces included between the arch and a square formed at the outside of it, are called *spandrells,* and are often ornamented.

Windows are divided into lights by *mullions.*

The ornaments of the divisions at the heads of windows, &c. are called *tracery.* Tracery is either *flowing,* where the lines branch out into the resemblance of leaves arches, and other figures ; or *perpendicular,* where the mullions are continued through in straight lines.

The horizontal divisions of windows and pannelling, are called *transoms.*

The parts of tracery are ornamented with small arches and points, which are called *featherings* or *foliations,* and the small arches *cusps;* and according to the number in immediate connexion, they are called *trefoils, quatrefoils,* or *cinquefoils.*

The cusps are sometimes again feathered, and this is called *double feathering.*

Tablets are small projecting mouldings, or strings, mostly horizontal.

The tablet at the top, under the battlement, is called a *cornice,* and that at the bottom a basement, under which is generally a thicker wall.

The tablet running round doors and windows, is called a *dripstone,* and if ornamented, a *canopy.*

Bands are either small strings round shafts, or a horizontal line of square, round, or other pannels, used to ornament towers, spires, and other works.

Niches are small arches, mostly sunk in the wall, often ornamented very richly with buttresses and canopies, and frequently containing statues.

A *corbel* is an ornamented projection from the wall.

to support an arch, niche, beam, or other apparent weight, and is often a head or part of a figure.

A *pinnacle* is a small spire, generally with four sides, and ornamented; it is usually placed on the tops of buttresses, both external and internal.

The small bunches of foliage ornamenting canopies and pinnacles, are called *crockets*.

The larger bunches on the top are called *finials,* and this term is sometimes applied to the whole pinnacle.

The seats for the dean, canons, and other dignitaries, in the choirs of collegiate churches, are called *stalls.*

The bishop's seat is called his *throne.*

The ornamented open work over the stalls, and in general any minute ornamental open work, is called *tabernacle work.*

In some churches, not collegiate, there yet remains a screen, with a large projection at the top, between the nave and chancel, on which was anciently placed certain images; this was called the *rood loft.*

Near the entrance door is sometimes found a small niche, with a basin which held, in catholic times, their holy water; these are called *stoups.*

Near the altar, or at least where an altar has once been placed, there is sometimes found another niche, distinguished from the stoup by having a small hole at the bottom to carry off water; it is often double, with a place for the bread.

On the south side, at the east end of some churches, are found stone stalls, either one, two, three, or sometimes more, of which the uses have been much contested. (*They were for the priest, deacon and subdeacon.—*)

Under several large churches, and some few small ones, are certain vaulted chapels, these are called *crypts.*

In order to render the comparison of the different styles easy, we shall divide the description of each into the following sections:

Doors,
Windows,

Arches,
Piers,
Buttresses,
Tablets,
Niches, and ornamental arches, or pannels,
Ornamental carvings,
Steeples, and
Battlements, roofs, fronts, and porches.

We shall first give, at one view, the date of the styles, and their most prominent distinctions, and then proceed to the particular sections as described above.

1st, the *Norman style*, which prevailed to the end of the reign of Henry II, in 1189 ; distinguished by its arches being generally semi-circular; though sometimes pointed, with bold and rude ornaments. This style seems to have commenced before the conquest, but we have no remains *really known* to be more than a very few years older.

2nd, the *Early English style*, reaching to the end of the reign of Edward I, in 1307 ; distinguished by pointed arches, and long narrow windows, without mullions; and a peculiar ornament, which, from its resemblance to the teeth of a shark, we shall hereafter call the toothed ornament.

3d, *Decorated English*, reaching to the end of the reign of Edward III, in 1377, and perhaps from ten to fifteen years longer. This style is distinguished by its large windows, which have pointed arches divided by mullions, and the tracery in flowing lines forming circles, arches, and other figures, not running perpendicularly; its ornaments numerous, and very delicately carved.

Perpendicular English. This is the last style, and appears to have been in use, though much debased, even as far as to 1630 or 1640, but only in additions. Probably the latest whole building is not later than Henry the VIII. The name clearly designates this style, for the mullions of the windows, and the ornamental pannellings, run in perpendicular lines, and form a complete distinction from the last style; and many buildings of this are so crowded with ornament, as to destroy the beauty of the design. The carvings are generally very delicately executed.

It may be necessary to state, that though many writers speak of Saxon buildings, those which they describe as such, are either known to be Norman, or are so like them, that there is no real distinction. But it is most likely, that in some obscure country church, some *real* Saxon work of a much earlier date may exist; hitherto, however, none has been ascertained to be of so great an age.

Without venturing to fix a date to either, it will be proper here to mention two towers which have hitherto been very little noticed, and yet are of very singular construction; the first is, that of the *old* church, St. Peter's, at Barton, in Lincolnshire; this is a short thick tower, with very thick walls, originally of three stages; the two lower of which are ornamented by perpendicular stripes of stone, projecting from the face of the wall, and near the top of each stage breaking into arches; the lower set of arches semi-circular, and the perpendicular lines springing from a stone set on the top of the arch; the second set are straight-lined arches, and run up to a flat string or tablet, on which is the third plain stage, with only two small arches, (if so they may be called,) as in the second stage. On the top of these three stages is one evidently early Norman, having a regular double Norman window in it, with a shaft and capital in the middle; this stage being clearly Norman, it is evident, the substructure must be of an earlier date; and in the second stage of the lower part is also a double window, with round arches, and divided by something (evidently original, for there are two) exactly resembling a rude balustre; all this arrangement is so different from Norman work, that there seems a probability it may be real Saxon; and it should be noted, that the other, or *new* church, St. Mary's, stands within 150 yards of the old church, and is principally a Norman building, with an Early English tower, and a chancel of the same ; and a very early Decorated east window, which, of course, renders it necessary to go back to the conquest at least, for the date of the old one. The other tower is that of Clapham church, in Bedfordshire ; and this is principally remarkable for the extreme simplicity and rudeness of its construction. It consists of a square tower, without buttress or tablet, about three squares high, with a rude round arch door, and above it two heights of small round arched windows; above this part of the tower, with a plain set-off, inwards is a Norman portion, with a Norman window divided into two by a central shaft, plain, and of early character ; this part is surmounted by a cornice and battlement of later date.

We shall now begin to trace the first or Norman style, and first of

NORMAN DOORS.

There seems to have been a desire in the architects who succeeded the Normans, to preserve the doors of their predecessors, whence we have so many of these noble, though, in most cases, rude efforts of skill remaining. In many small churches, where all has been swept away, to make room for alterations, even in the perpendicular style, the Norman door has been suffered to remain. The arch is semi-circular, and the mode of increasing their richness, was by increasing the number of bands of moulding, and, of course, the depth of the arch. Shafts are often used, but not always, and we find very frequently, in the same building, one door with shafts, and one without. When shafts are used, there is commonly an impost moulding above them, before the arch mouldings spring. These mouldings are generally much ornamented, and the wave or zigzag ornament, in some of its diversities, is almost universal, as is a large round moulding, with heads on the outer edge, partly projecting over this moulding. There are also mouldings with a series of figures enclosed in a running ornament; and at one church at York, these figures are the zodiacal signs. The exterior moulding often goes down no lower than the spring of the arch, thus forming an apparent dripstone, though it does not always project so as really to form one. The door is often square, and the interval to the arch filled with carvings. Amongst the great variety of these doors in excellent preservation, Iffley church, near Oxford, is perhaps the best specimen, as it contains three doors, all of which are different; and the south door is nearly unique, from the flowers in its interior mouldings. South Ockenden church, in Essex, has also a door of uncommon beauty of design, and elegance of execution. Ely, Durham, Rochester, Worcester, and Lincoln cathedrals, have also fine Norman doors. In these doors, almost all the ornament is external, and the inside often quite plain.

Almost every county in England contains many Norman doors; they are very often the only part which patching and altering has left worth examining, and they are remarkably varied, scarcely any two being alike. In delicacy of execution, and intricacy of design, the College Gate, at Bristol, seems equal, if not superior, to most; and indeed is so well worked, that some persons have been inclined to ascribe it to a later date; but an attentive examination of many other Norman works will show designs as intricate, where there can be no doubt of the date.

Norman Windows.

The windows, in this style, are diminutive doors as to their ornaments, except that, in large buildings, shafts are more frequent, and often with plain mouldings. The size of these windows is generally small, except in very large buildings; there are no mullions, but a double window divided by a shaft, is not uncommon. In small rich churches, the exterior is often a series of arches, of which a few are pierced, as windows, and the others left blank. The arch is semicircular, and if the window is quite plain, has generally sloped sides, either inside or out, or both. The proportions of the Norman windows are generally those of a door, and very rarely exceed two squares in height of the exterior proportions, including the ornaments.

The existing Norman windows are mostly in buildings retaining still the entire character of that style; for in most they have been taken out, and others of later styles put in, as at Durham, and many other cathedrals.

There are still remaining traces of a very few circular windows of this style; the west window at Iffley was circular, but it has been taken out; there is one in Canterbury cathedral, which seems to be Norman; and there is one undoubtedly Norman at Barfreston, rendered additionally singular by its being divided by grotesque heads, and something like mullions, though very rude, into eight parts.

There seems to have been little if any attempt at feathering or foliating the heads of Norman doors or windows.

Norman Arches.

The early Norman arches are semi-circular, and in many instances this form of the arch seems to have continued to the latest date, even when some of the parts were quite advanced into the next style; of this the temple church is a curious instance; here are piers with some of the features of the next style, and also pointed arches with a range of intersecting arches, and over this, the old round-headed Norman window. But though the round arch thus continued to the very end of the style, the introduction of pointed arches must have been much earlier, for we find intersecting arches in buildings of the purest Norman, and whoever constructed them, constructed pointed arches; but it appears as if the round and pointed arches were, for nearly a century, used indiscriminately, as was most consonant to the necessities of the work, or the builder's ideas. Kirkstall and Buildwas abbeys, have all their exterior round arches, but the nave has pointed arches in the interior. There are some Norman arches so near a semi-circle as to be only just perceptibly pointed, and with the rudely carved Norman ornaments.

There are a few Norman arches of very curious shape, being more than a semi-circle, or what is called a horse-shoe, and in a few instances a double arch. These arches are sometimes plain, but are much oftener enriched with the zigzag, and other ornaments peculiar to this style.

NORMAN PIERS.

These are of four descriptions, 1st, The round massive columnar pier, which has sometimes a round, and sometimes a square capital; they are generally plain, but sometimes ornamented with channels in various forms, some plain zigzag, some like network, and some spiral. They are sometimes met with but little more than two diameters high, and sometimes are six or seven.

2d, A multangular pier, much less massive, is sometimes used, generally octagonal, and commonly with an arch more or less pointed.

3d, The common pier with shafts; these have sometimes plain capitals, but are sometimes much ornamented with rude foliage, and occasionally animals. The shafts are mostly set in square recesses.

4th, A plain pier, with perfectly plain round arches, in two or three divisions.

In some cases, the shafts are divided by bands, but the instances are not many.

Norman Buttresses.

These require little description; they are plain, broad faces, with but small projection, often only a few inches, and running up only to the cornice tablet, and there finishing under its projection. Sometimes they are finished with a plain slope, and in a few instances are composed of several shafts. Bands or tablets running along the walls, often run round the buttresses. There are, however, in rich buildings, buttresses ornamented with shafts at the angles, and in addition to these shafts, small series of arches are sometimes used; occasionally a second buttress, of less breadth, is placed on the outside of the broad flat one.

Norman Tablets.

In treating of tablets, that which is usually called the cornice, is of the first consideration; this is frequently only a plain face of parapet, of the same projection as the buttresses; but a row of blocks is often placed under it, sometimes plain, sometimes carved in grotesque heads, and in some instances the grotesque heads support small arches, when it is called a corbel table. A plain string is also sometimes used as a cornice.

The next most important tablet is the dripstone, or outer moulding of windows and doors; this is sometimes undistinguished, but oftener a square string, frequently continued horizontally from one window to another, round the buttresses.

The tablets, under windows, are generally plain slopes above or below a flat string. In the interior, and in some instances in the exterior, these are much carved in the various ornaments described hereafter.

Norman Niches, &c.

These are a series of small arches with round and often with intersecting arches, sometimes without, but oftener with shafts. Some of these arches have their mouldings much ornamented.

There are also other niches of various shapes over doors, in which are placed figures; they are generally of small depth, and most of them retain the figures originally placed in them.

Norman Ornaments.

The ornaments of this style consist principally of the different kinds of carved mouldings surrounding doors and windows, and used as tablets. The first and most frequent of them, is the zigzag or chevron moulding, which is generally used in great profusion. The next most common on door mouldings, is the beak-head moulding, consisting of a hollow and a large round; in the hollow are placed heads of beasts or birds, whose tongues or beaks encircle the round. After these come many varieties, almost every specimen having some difference of composition; a good collection of them may be seen in the Archæologia, and King's Munimenta Antiqua.

The capitals of piers and shafts are often very rudely carved in various grotesque devices of animals and leaves, but in all the design is rude and the plants are unnatural.

There is one moulding which deserves mention, from its almost constant occurrence, very nearly of the same pattern and proportions over every part of the kingdom; this is the moulding of the square abacus, over the flowered or cut part of the capital; it consists of a broad fillet and hollow, which are separated by a little sunk channel, and it is sometimes continued as a tablet along the walls.

Norman Steeples.

The Norman steeple was mostly a massive tower, seldom rising more than a square in height above the roof of the building to which it belonged, and often not so much. They are sometimes plain, but often ornamented by plain or intersecting arches, and have generally the flat buttress, but that of St. Alban's runs into a round turret at each corner of the upper stage, and at St. Peter's, Northampton, there is a singular buttress of three parts of circles, but its date is uncertain. The towers of Norwich and Winchester cathedrals, and Tewksbury church, are very fine specimens of the Norman tower. It does not seem likely that we have any Norman spires, but there are some turrets crowned with large pinnacles, which may be Norman—such is one at Cleve, in Gloucestershire, and one of the towers at the side of the west front of Rochester cathedral.

Norman Battlements.

From exposure to weather, and various accidents, we find very few roofs in their original state, and from the vicinity of the battlement we find this part also very often not original. It seems difficult to ascertain what the Norman battlement was, and there seems much reason to suppose it was only a plain parapet; in some castellated Norman buildings, a parapet, with here and there a narrow interval cut in it, remains, and appears original; and this, or the plain parapet, was most likely the ecclesiastical battlement. Many Norman buildings have battlements of much later date, or parapets evidently often repaired.

53

Norman Roofs.

The Norman wooden roof was often open to the actual frame-timbers, as we see some remaining to this day, as at Rochester and Winchester; but at Peterborough is a real flat boarded cieling, which is in fine preservation, having lately been carefully repainted from the original. It consists of a sort of rude Mosaic, full of stiff lines; and its general division is into lozenges, with flowers of Norman character, and the whole according in design with the ornaments of that style. This kind of roof, particularly when the exterior was covered with shingles, contributed much to spread those destructive fires we so frequently read of in the history of early churches. Of the Norman groined roof, we have very many fine examples, principally in the roofs of crypts, and in small churches; they consist of cross springers, and sometimes, but not always, of a rib from pier to pier; they are sometimes plain, but oftener ornamented with ribs of a few bold mouldings, and sometimes with these mouldings enriched with zigzag and other carved work of this style. The ruins of Landisfarne, on the Northumberland coast, have long exhibited the great cross springer rib, over the intersection of the nave and transepts, remaining while the rest of the roof is destroyed.

Norman Fronts.

The greatest part of the Norman west fronts have been much changed by the introduction of windows of later date (mostly large perpendicular windows.) The ruins of Landisfarne, however, present us with one nearly perfect. This consists of a large door with a gallery or triforium over it, of which some of the arches have been pierced through for windows; and above, one larger window. Rochester and Lincoln cathedrals, Castle Acre priory, and Tewksbury church, all show what the Norman west fronts were, with the exception of the introduction of the large window. The east fronts much resembled the west, except the door; and in small churches we have both east and west fronts perfect. Peterborough and Winchester cathedrals furnish fine examples (except the insertion of tracery to the windows) of transept ends; these generally rose in three tiers of windows, and had a fine effect, both interiorly and exteriorly. There are a few large buildings, and many small ones, with semi-circular east ends; and of these, the east ends of Norwich and Peterborough cathedrals are the finest remaining, but in both, the windows are altered by the insertion of tracery, and in parts, of new windows.

NORMAN PORCHES.

There are many of these remaining to small churches; they are generally shallow, and the mouldings of the outer gate are often richer than those of the inner.

The general appearance of Norman buildings is bold and massive. Very few large buildings remain without much alteration and mixture with other styles; perhaps the nave at Peterborough and that of Rochester cathedrals, present as little mixture as any, though in these the windows have been altered; but of smaller churches, Barfreston in Kent, Stewkley in Buckinghamshire, and Adel in Yorkshire, have had very little alteration. Tickencote, in Rutland, till within a few years, was one of the most valuable remains in the kingdom; but it has been rebuilt sufficiently near in its likeness to the original to deceive many, and so far from it as to render it not a copy, but an imitation; yet it is still curious, and the interior of the chancel is original. The interior arrangement of large Norman buildings is considerably varied: sometimes the large circular pier is used alone, as at Gloucester cathedral; sometimes mixed with the pier composed of shafts, as at Durham; and sometimes of that pier

of shafts only, as at Peterborough, Norwich, &c.—
The triforia are various; some, as at Southwell and
Waltham abbey, a large arch quite open, but oftener
broken by small shafts and arches, and the clerestory
windows have often an arch on each side of the window,
forming a second gallery; of these galleries, which are
partly pierced, the tower of Norwich forms the best
example. In many large churches we find the Norman
work remaining only to the string running over the
arches, and later work above that; this is the case at
Canterbury and Hereford. The arrangement at Oxford
cathedral is curious, as under the great arches,
springing from the piers, are other arches springing
from corbels, and between these two are shafts and
arches as ornaments, but not open as a gallery. In
small churches the gallery is generally omitted.

Of this style, it will be proper to remark two
buildings that deserve attention; the one for its simplicity and beauty of composition, the other from its
being nearly unique, and being at the same time
a very fine specimen of ornament. The first is the
vestibule, or entrance to the chapter-house, at Bristol,
and the other the staircase leading to the registry at
Canterbury cathedral. With respect to ornaments,
few surpass those of a ruined tower at Canterbury,
generally called Ethelbert's, and those on the front of
Castle Acre priory. Norman fronts are very numerous,
perhaps as much so as Norman doors, and some
are very curious from the rudeness and intricacy of
the decorations. There are many fine Norman castellated remains; of these it may be enough to mention
those of Rochester in Kent, Hedingham in Essex,
Connisburgh in Yorkshire, and Guildford in Surrey.

The transition from Norman to Early English was
gradual, and it is sometimes very difficult to decide
on the character of some remains; in general, the
square abacus to the capital is the best mark, for the
arch is none, many pure Norman works having the
pointed arch. The mouldings of later Norman work

approach very near to Early English. The Temple
church, London, is one of those buildings which seems
to belong as much to one style as the other; and two
Lincolnshire buildings, not far distant from each other,
show a curious crossing of the marks of these two
styles:—one, the front of the hospital of St. Leonard,
at Stamford, presents a semi-circular arch with pure
Norman mouldings, but the shafts are in two rows,
stand free, and have a round abacus of several mouldings, which are quite Early English. The other, part
of Ketton church, has the square Norman abacus and
semi-circular arch with Norman mouldings, and another
pointed one on the side ; but both these have a dripstone filled with the toothed ornament, which also runs
down by the shafts, which are banded and have an
Early English base.

Of the Second, or Early English Style.

EARLY ENGLISH DOORS.

As the Norman doors may be said to be all of semi-
circular arches, these may be said to be all pointed, at
least all the exterior ornamented ones; for there are
small interior doors of this style with flat tops, and
the sides of the top supported by a quarter circle from
each side. The large doors of this style are often
double, the two being divided by either one shaft or
several clustered, and a quatrefoil or other ornament
over them. The recess of these doors is often as deep
as the Norman, but the bands and shafts are more
numerous, being smaller ; and in the hollow mouldings they are frequently enriched with the peculiar
ornament of this style—a singular toothed projection,
which, when well executed, has a fine effect. But
although this ornament is often used, (and sometimes
a still higher enriched moulding, or band of open-work

flowers,) there are many doors of this style perfectly plain; of this kind the door of Christ church, Hants, is a fine specimen.

The dripstone is generally clearly marked, and often small, and supported by a head. In many doors, a trefoil, and even cinquefoil feathering is used, the points of which generally finish with balls, roses, or some projecting ornament. The principal moulding of these doors has generally an equilateral arch, but from the depth and number of the mouldings, the exterior becomes often nearly a semi-circle. In interiors, and perhaps sometimes too in the exterior, there are instances of doors with a trefoil-headed arch. The shafts attached to these doors are generally round, but sometimes filleted, and they generally, but not always, stand quite free. They have a variety of capitals, many plain, but many with delicate leaves running up and curling round under the cap-moulding, often looking like Ionic volutes. The bases are various, but a plain round and fillet is often used, and the reversed ogee sometimes introduced. The most prevalent base, and what is used not only to shafts, but sometimes as a base tablet, is curious, from its likeness to the Grecian attic base; like that it consists of two rounds, with a hollow between, and that hollow is often deepened, so that if water gets into it the water remains, and it is almost the only instance of a moulding used in English work which will hold water, they being in general so constructed as entirely to free themselves of rain, and in a great measure of snow. All these mouldings are cut with great boldness, the hollows form fine deep shadows, and the rich bands of open-work leaves are as beautiful as those executed at any subsequent period, being sometimes entirely hollow, and having no support but the attachment at the sides, and the connexion of the leaves themselves. These doors are not so numerous as the Norman, yet many still remain in perfect preservation—York, Lincoln, Chichester, and Salisbury, have extremely fine ones, and Beverley minster one, of which the mouldings are bolder than most others. The door of the transept at York, and those of the choir-screen at Lincoln, have bands of the richest execution, and there is a fine double door at St. Cross. Litchfield cathedral presents a door curious for its resemblance to some foreign cathedrals; it is placed in a shallow porch formed in the thickness of the wall, the arch of which is richly feathered, and otherwise ornamented; the interior aperture is divided into two doorways by a pier of shafts, and this pier, as well as the side piers of both the apertures, has a statue fixed against it, resting on a corbel, and crowned with a canopy. The recess is groined, and the whole is worked with great delicacy, and full of rich ornament; the interior portion is in tolerable preservation, the exterior much decayed; the doors appear original, and are covered with beautiful ramifications of scroll-work, in iron. Indeed there are many wooden doors, both of this style and Norman, which seem to be of the same age as the stone-work.

EARLY ENGLISH WINDOWS.

These are, almost universally, long, narrow, and lancet-headed, generally without feathering, but in some instances trefoiled.

A variety of appearance results from the combination of this single shape of window. At Salisbury, one of the earliest complete buildings remaining, there are combinations of two, three, five, and seven. Where there are two, there is often a trefoil or quatrefoil between the heads; and in large buildings, where there are three or more, the division is often so small that they seem to be the lights of a large window, but they are really separate windows, having their heads formed from individual centres, and in general separate dripstones. This is the case even at Westminster, where they approach nearer to a division by mullions, from having a small triangle pierced beside the quatrefoil, and a general dripstone over all. It appears that the double window, with a circle over it, sometimes pierced and sometimes not, began to be used early in the style, for we find it at Salisbury; and this continued the ornamented window till the latest period of the style; it was indeed only making a double door into a window. In the more advanced period it was doubled into a four-light window — at Salisbury, in the cloisters and chapter-house; and the east window of Lincoln cathedral is of eight lights, formed by doubling the four-light, still making the circle the ornament. This window is in fact a Decorated window, but together with the whole of that part of the choir is singularly and beautifully accommodated to the style of the rest of the building. In small buildings, the windows are generally plain, with the slope of the opening considerable, and in some small chapels they are very narrow and long. In large buildings they are often ornamented with very long and slender shafts, which are frequently banded. Most of our cathedrals contain traces of windows of this character, but some, as at Durham, have tracery added since their original erection. Salisbury, Chichester, Lincoln, Beverley, and York, still remain pure and beautiful; at York north transept are windows nearly fifty feet high, and about six or eight wide, which have a very fine effect. Although the architects of this style worked their ordinary windows thus plain, they bestowed much care on their circles. Beverley minster, York and Lincoln, have all circles of this style peculiarly fine; that of the south transept at York, usually called the marygold window, is extremely rich, but the tracery of the circles at Westminster is of a much later date.

There is in all the long windows of this style, one almost universal distinction; from the straight side of the window opening, if a shaft is added, it is mostly insular, and has seldom any connexion with this side, so as to break it into faces, though the shafts are inserted into the sides of the doors, so as to give great variety to the opening.

At Westminster abbey, there are a series of windows above those of the aisles, which are formed in spherical equilateral triangles.

EARLY ENGLISH ARCHES.

The window-arch of this style being generally a lancet arch, and some persons having considered the shape of the arch to be a very distinguishing feature of the different styles, it may be necessary in this place to say a few words on arches generally. If we examine with care the various remains of the different styles, we shall see no such constancy of arch as has been apprehended; for there are composition lancet arches used both at Henry the VII.'s chapel Westminster, and at Bath; and there are flat segmental arches in the Early English part of York; and upon the whole it will appear, that the architect was not confined to any particular description of arch. The only arch precisely attached to one period, is the four-centred arch, which does not appear in windows, &c. if it does in composition, before the Perpendicular style. In large buildings, the nave arches of the Early English style were often lancet, but in some large and many small ones, they are flatter, some of one-third drop, and perhaps even more, and sometimes pointed segmental.

At Canterbury, in the choir, are some curious pointed horse-shoe arches, but these are not common.

The architraves of the large arches of rich buildings are now beautifully moulded like the doors, with deep, hollow mouldings, often enriched with the toothed ornament. Of this description, York transepts, and the nave and transepts of Lincoln, are beautiful specimens; Salisbury is worked plainer, but not less really beautiful, and Westminster abbey is (the nave at least) nearly plain, but with great boldness of moulding.

The arches of the gallery in this style, are often with trefoiled heads, and the mouldings running round the trefoil, even to the dripstone ; Chester choir is a fine specimen, and there are some plain arches of this description in Winchester cathedral which are very beautiful.

EARLY ENGLISH PIERS.

Of the piers of large buildings of this style, there are two distinguishing marks ; first, the almost constant division, by one or more bands, of the shafts which compose them; and secondly, the arrangement of these shafts for the most part in a circle.   In general they are few, sometimes only four, sometimes eight, set round a large circular one ; such are the piers of Salisbury and of Westminster abbey ; there are sometimes so many as nearly to hide the centre shaft, as at Lincoln and York ; but the circular arrangement is still preserved, and there are some few, as at the choir at Chester, which come very near the appearance of Decorated piers.   Amongst other piers, one not very common deserves to be noticed; it is found at Beverley minster, and in a few other churches; it consists of shafts, some of which are plain rounds, others filleted rounds, and some whose plan is a spherical triangle, with the edge outwards ; at Runcorn church, Cheshire, is a pier consisting of four of these triangular shafts, with a handsome flowered capital, which has altogether a very fine effect.

The capitals of these shafts are various ; in many, perhaps the greater number of buildings, they are plain, consisting of a bell with a moulding under it, and a sort of capping, with more mouldings above, and these mouldings are often continued round the centre pier, so as to form a general capital.   The dividing bands are formed of annulets and fillets, and are often continued under windows, &c. as tablets, and are, like the capitals, sometimes continued round the centre shaft. Another and richer capital is some-times used, which has leaves like those in the capitals of the door shafts. This kind of capital is generally used where the shafts entirely encompass the centre one, as at York and Lincoln, and has a very fine effect, the leaves being generally extremely well executed. The bases used are frequently near approaches in contour to the Grecian attic base, but the reversed ogee is sometimes employed. There is another pier, in buildings that appear to be of this style, which is at times very confusing, as the same kind of pier seems to be used in small churches even to a very late date; this is the plain multangular (generally octagonal) pier, with a plain capital of a few very simple mouldings, and with a plain sloped arch. Piers of this description are very frequent, and it requires great nicety of observation and discrimina-tion to refer them to their proper date; but a minute examination will often, by some small matter, detect their age, though it is impossible to describe the minutiæ without many figures. In general the capitals and bases will carry in their character sufficient marks to determine their date, except in the transition from Early English to Decorated.

EARLY ENGLISH BUTTRESSES.

These are of four descriptions:

1st. A flat buttress is often used, but it is not always so broad as the Norman; its tablets are more delicate, and it has often the small shaft at the angle like the Norman.

2nd. A buttress not so broad as the flat one, but nearly of the same projection as breadth, and carried up, sometimes with only one set-off, and sometimes without any, and these have often their edges chamfered from the window tablet. They sometimes have a shaft at the corner, and in large rich buildings are occasionally pannelled. These buttresses have also, at times, much more projection than breadth, and are sometimes, as at Salisbury, filled with niches and other ornaments.

3d. A long slender buttress, of narrow face and great projection in few stages, is used in some towers, but is not very common.

4th. Towards the latter part of this style, the buttress in stages was used, but it is not very common, and is sufficiently distinguished by its triangular head, the usual finish of this style, which can hardly be called a pinnacle, though sometimes it slopes off from the front to a point. From the buttresses of the aisles to those of the nave, choir, &c. now began to be used the flying buttress, of which Salisbury and Chichester cathedrals present various fine examples.

Early English Tablets.

The cornice is sometimes rich in mouldings, and often with an upper slope, making the face of the parapet perpendicular to the wall below. There are cornices of this style still resembling the Norman projecting parapet, but they consist of several mould ings. The hollow moulding of the cornice is generally plain, seldom containing flowers or carvings, *except the toothed ornament*, but under the mouldings there is often a series of small arches resembling the corbel table.

The dripstone of this style is various, sometimes of several mouldings, sometimes only a round with a small hollow. It is, in the interior, occasionally ornamented with the toothed ornament, and with flowers. In some buildings, the dripstone is returned, and runs as a tablet along the walls. It is in general narrow, and supported by a corbel, either of a head or a flower. There are frequently, in large buildings, in the ornamented parts, bands of trefoils, quatrefoils, &c. some of them very rich. Although a

64

sort of straight canopy is used over some of the niches
of this style, yet it does not appear to have been used
over windows or doors. In some buildings where they
are found, they appear to be additions. The tablets
forming the base-mouldings are sometimes a mere
slope; at others, in large buildings, are of several sets
of mouldings, each face projecting farther than the
one above it; but the reversed ogee is very seldom
used, at least at large and singly.

EARLY ENGLISH NICHES.

The most important niches are those found in
chancels, in the walls of the south side, and of which
the uses do not yet appear to be decided. Of these
there are many of all stages of Early English; there
are sometimes two, but oftener three, and they are
generally sunk in the wall, and adapted for a seat; the
easternmost one is often higher in the seat than the
others. They have sometimes a plain trefoil head,
and are sometimes ornamented with shafts; they are
generally straight-sided. The statuary niches, and
ornamented interior niches, mostly consist of a series
of arches, some of them slope-sided, and some with a
small but not very visible pedestal for the statue.
They are often grouped two under one arch, with an
ornamental opening between the small arches, and the
large one like the double doors; a straight-sided
canopy is sometimes used, and a plain finial. These
niches, except the chancel stalls, and the stoup and
water-drain, are seldom single, except in buttresses, but
mostly in ranges.

EARLY ENGLISH ORNAMENTS.

The first ornament to be described is that already
noticed as the peculiar distinction of this style, to
which it seems nearly, if not exclusively confined; it is
the regular progression from the Norman zigzag to

the delicate four-leaved flowers so common in Decorated English buildings. Like the zigzag, it is generally straight-sided, and not round like the leaves of a flower, though, at a distance in front, it looks much like a small flower. It is very difficult to describe it, and still more so to draw it accurately; it may perhaps be understood by considering it a succession of low, square, pierced pyramids, set on the edges of a hollow moulding. This ornament is used very profusely in the buildings of this style, in Yorkshire and Lincolnshire, and frequently in those of other counties.

Another ornament, which, though not peculiar, in small works, to this style, was seldom but during its continuance practised to so large an extent; this is the filling of the spaces above the choir-arches with squares, enclosing four-leaved flowers. This is done at Westminster, at Chichester, and in the screen at Lincoln, in all which the workmanship is extremely good, and it has a very rich effect.

In many parts, as in the spandrels of door-arches, and other plain spaces, circles filled with trefoils and quatrefoils, with flowered points, are often introduced. These are of small depth, and are used in many buildings very freely. Sometimes instead of sunk pannels a sort of boss of leaves and flowers is used, of which there are some fine examples in the Early English part of York minster. In the early period of the style, crockets were not used, and the finial was a plain bunch of three or more leaves, or sometimes only a sort of knob; but in small rich works, towards the end of the style, beautiful finials and crockets were introduced.

EARLY ENGLISH STEEPLES.

The Norman towers were short and thick, the Early English rose to a much greater height, and on the tower they placed that beautiful addition the spire.

F

Some of our finest spires are of this age, and the proportions observed between the tower and spire, are generally very good. Chichester is clearly of this style, and Salisbury, though perhaps not erected till within the period of the Decorated style, is yet in its composition so completely of Early English character, that it should be considered as such, notwithstanding the date and the advance of its ornaments; in beauty of proportion it is unrivalled. The towers of Lincoln and Litchfield, though perhaps not finished within the date of the style, are yet of its composition; the spires of Litchfield are of much later date. Wakefield steeple is finely proportioned, though plain, and it is singular for its machicolations in the top of the tower. The towers are flanked by octagonal turrets, square flat buttresses, or, in a few instances, with small long buttresses; and generally there is one large octagonal pinnacle at the corners, or a collection of small niches. When there is no parapet, the slope of the spire runs down to the edge of the wall of the tower, and finishes there with a tablet; and there is a double slope to connect the corners with the intermediate faces. The spire is often ornamented by ribs at the angles, some-times with crockets on the ribs, and bands of squares filled with quatrefoils, &c. surrounding the spire at different heights. There are many good spires of this style in country churches.

EARLY ENGLISH BATTLEMENTS.

During nearly the whole of this style, the parapet, in many places plain, in others ornamented, continued to be used; at Salisbury it has a series of arches and pannels, and at Lincoln quatrefoils in sunk pannels. Perhaps some of the earliest battlement is that at the west end of Salisbury cathedral, plain, of nearly equal intervals, and with a plain capping moulding; but it may be doubted if even this is original. In small ornamented works, of the latter part of this style, a small battlement of equal intervals occurs

Early English Roofs.

The roof of the nave of Salisbury cathedral presents the best specimen of Early English groined roof; it has cross springers, and the rib from pier to pier, but it has no rib running longitudinally or across at the point of the arches. Another description of groining, also peculiar to Early English works, is one with an additional rib between the cross springer and the wall, and between the cross springer and the pier rib; this has a longitudinal and cross rib at the point of the arches, but it does not run to the wall, being stopt by the intermediate rib. The old groining, in a passage out of the cloisters, at Chester, is a very good specimen of this roof. Another variety is found at Litchfield, where there is no pier rib, but the two intermediate ribs are brought nearer together, and the longitudinal rib runs between them. The rib mouldings of these groins are not very large, and consist of rounds and hollows, and often have the toothed ornament in them, and at Litchfield a sort of leaf. The bosses in these roofs are not many or very large, the intersections being frequently plain, but some of the bosses are very well worked. There do not appear to be any Early English wooden roofs which can clearly be distinguished to be such.

Early English Fronts.

There is, perhaps, a greater variety in the Early English fronts, than in those of any other style; the west front of Salisbury is, no doubt, the finest; but the transept ends of Salisbury, York, and Beverley, are very fine, and all different in composition. The ruins of Tynemouth priory, Valle Crucis abbey, Byland abbey, and Whitby abbey, all exhibit the remains of excellent work. Of the smaller works the east end of the lady-chapel at Salisbury, the extreme

east end of Hereford cathedral, and the north transept
of Headon church, near Hull, deserve attention. In
general the west fronts and transept ends have a door,
and one, two, three, or even four ranges of niches,
windows, and arches over them. The transepts of
Westminster abbey are very fine, but much of the
work is not original. The west front of Lincoln
minster deserves minute examination for its details;
the old Norman front is encompassed by Early English,
the workmanship of which is very superior; and a
large feathered circle over the great door is nearly
unique, from the exquisite workmanship of its mouldings, which consist of open-work bands of flowers.
The west front of Peterborough cathedral is different
from all the rest; it consists of three large arches,
forming a sort of screen to the front. These arches
have piers of many shafts, and fine architraves, and
the gables enriched with much small work of circles
and arches, and a profusion of the toothed ornament
over the whole.

EARLY ENGLISH PORCHES.

Of these, which are in general larger than the
Norman porches, it will be sufficient to mention two;
one the north porch of Salisbury cathedral, and the
other the south porch at Lincoln. The first is
attached to the north side of the nave, of which it
occupies one division, rising as high as the aisles; it
consists of a noble plain arched entrance, over which
are two double windows, close together, resting
on a tablet; and quite in the peak of the gable, two
small niches close together resting on another string.
The interior is groined in two divisions, and its walls
ornamented with sunk pannelling. The porch at Lincoln is placed in a singular situation, running westerly
from the west side of the south transept. The lower
part is a rich piece of groined work, with three
entrances — north, south, and west, over which is a

small room; the whole of this porch, both interior and exterior, is well worked, and richly ornamented.

The general appearance of Early English building is magnificent, and rich rather from the number of parts than from its details. In those buildings where very long windows are used, there is a grandeur arising from the height of the divisions; in smaller buildings there is much simplicity of appearance, and there is a remarkable evenness in the value of the workmanship. There is much of the other styles which appears evidently to be the copy by an inferior hand of better workmanship elsewhere; this is remarkably the case in Perpendicular work, but is hardly any where to be found in Early English work, all appears well designed and carefully executed.

Of this style we have the great advantage of one building remaining, worked in its best manner, of great size and in excellent preservation; this is Salisbury cathedral, and it gives a very high idea of the great improvement of this style on the Norman. Magnificent without rudeness, and rich, though simple, it is one uniform whole. The west front is ornamented, but by no means loaded, and the appearance of the north side is perhaps equal to the side of any cathedral in England. The west front of Lincoln is fine, but the old Norman space is too visible not to break it into parts. Peterborough and Ely have perhaps the most ornamented fronts of this style. As interiors, after Salisbury, the transepts of York are perhaps the best specimens, though there are parts of many other buildings deserving much attention.

In the interior arrangement of large buildings we find the triforium a very prominent feature; it is large in proportion to the work above and below it, and is generally the most ornamented part of the work. In small churches the triforium is generally omitted. Among the greatest beauties of this style are some of the chapter-houses, of which Lincoln and Litchfield, both decagons, but of very different arrangement;

and those of Chester and Oxford, both parallelograms, deserve particular attention; but that of Salisbury, a regular octagon, and of a character quite late in the style, is one of the most beautiful buildings remaining. Its composition is peculiarly elegant, and its execution not excelled by any.

There appear to be fewer fonts of this style remaining than of any other, at least of such as can be clearly marked as belonging to the style.

Not much has been done in either restoring or imitating this style; it is certainly not easy to do either well, but it deserves attention, as in many places it would be peculiarly appropriate, and perhaps is better fitted than any for small country churches. It may be worked almost entirely plain, yet if ornament is used, it should be well executed; for the ornaments of this style are in general as well executed as any of later date, and the toothed ornament and hollow bands equal, in difficulty of execution, the most elaborate Perpendicular ornaments.

If the transition from Norman to Early English was gradual, much more so was that from Early English to Decorated ; and we have several curious examples of this transition on a large scale. Westminster abbey, though carried on for a long time, appears to have been carefully continued on the original design; and except a very few parts, some of which are quite modern, may be considered good Early English throughout; but in the cloisters there is much gradation. Ely cathedral presents Early English of several dates, from just clear of Norman to almost Decorated character. The nave of Litchfield, though clearly Early English in composition, has the windows of the aisles as clearly Decorated. Perhaps the finest piece of accommodation between the styles is the lady-chapel at Lincoln, which is evidently Decorated, but executed so as beautifully to harmonize with the work about it.

Early English staircases (except round ones in towers) are not common; it is proper therefore to remark a small one, of rich character, at Beverley minster; it leads from the north aisle of the choir to some adjacent building, and consists of a series of arches rising each higher than the former, with elegant shafts and mouldings. There is another in the refectory (now a grammar-school) at Chester, leading up to a large niche or sort of pulpit, for the reader.

In this style ought to be noticed those beautiful monuments of conjugal affection, the crosses of Queen Eleanor. Of these, three remain sufficiently perfect to be restored, if required, and to do which little would be wanted to two of them. One at Geddington in Northamptonshire, is comparatively plain, but those of Northampton and Waltham are peculiarly rich, and of elegant composition; there is enough of Early English character in them to mark their date, and enough of Decorated richness to entitle them to be ranked as buildings of that style; that of Northampton is the most perfect, but that at Waltham is, on the whole, the most beautiful in its details.

There are few, if any, castellated remains in which this style can be clearly made out,

---

Of the Third, or Decorated English Style.

DECORATED ENGLISH DOORS.

The large doors of the last style are mostly double, and there are some fine ones of this, but they are not so common, there being more single doors, which are often nearly as large as the Early English double ones, and indeed but for the ornaments they are much alike, having shafts and fine hollow mouldings. The small doors are frequently without shafts, but the arch-mouldings run down the side, and almost to the ground, without a base,—the mouldings being set upon a slope, and frequently, when the base tablets consist of two sets of mouldings with a face between, it is only the lower one which runs into the architrave to stop the mouldings. The shafts do not in this style generally stand free, but are parts of the sweep of mouldings; and instead of being cut and set up lengthways, all the mouldings and shafts are cut on the arch-stone, thus combining great strength with all the appearance of lightness. The capitals of these shafts differ from the Early English, in being formed of a woven foliage, and not upright leaves; this, in small shafts, generally has an apparent neck, but in larger ones often appears like a round ball of open foliage. There are also, in many good buildings, plain capitals without foliage; these have an increased number of mouldings from those of the last style, and they generally consist of three sets, — one which may be considered the abacus, then a hollow and another set, then the bell of the capital, and then the mouldings forming the astragal: and both in plain and flowered capitals, where the shaft is filleted, it is common for the fillet to run through the astragal, and appear to die into the bell. Of these plain capitals, the cathedral of Exeter, and the cloisters of Norwich, furnish very fine specimens. The bases to these shafts mostly consist of the reversed ogee, but other mouldings are often added, and the ogee made in faces. Although the doors in general are not so deeply recessed, as the Norman and Early English, yet in many large buildings they are very deep. The west doors of York are of the richest execution, and very deep.

To the open-work bands of the last style, succeeds an ornament equally beautiful, and not so fragile; this is the flowered moulding; there are often three or four in one door-way, and to the toothed ornament succeeds a flower of four leaves, in a deep moulding, with considerable intervals between. This flower, in some buildings, is used in great profusion to good effect. Over these doors, there are several sorts of canopies; the dripstone is generally supported by a corbel, which is commonly a head; in some instances a plain return is used, but that return seldom runs horizontally. The canopy is sometimes connected with the dripstone, and sometimes distinct. The common canopy is a triangle, the space between it and the dripstone is filled with tracery, and the exterior ornamented with crockets, and crowned with a finial. The second canopy is the ogee, which runs about half up the dripstone, and then is turned the contrary way, and is finished in a straight line running up into a finial. This has its intermediate space filled with tracery, &c. and is generally crocketed. Another sort of canopy is an arch running over the door, and unconnected with it, which is doubly foliated; it has a good effect, but is not common. On the side of the doors, small buttresses or niches are sometimes placed.

In small churches, there are often nearly plain doors, having only a dripstone and a round moulding on the interior edge, and the rest of the wall a straight line or bold hollow, and in some instances a straight sloping side only. In some doors of this style, a series of niches with statues are carried up like a hollow moulding; and in others, doubly foliated tracery, hanging free from one of the outer mouldings, gives a richness superior to any other decoration. The south door of the choir at Lincoln is perhaps hardly any where equalled of the first kind, and a door in the cloisters of Norwich of the other.

DECORATED ENGLISH WINDOWS.

In these, the clearest marks of the style are to be found, and they are very various, yet all on one principle. An arch is divided by one or more mullions, into two or more lights, and these mullions branch into tracery of various figures, but do not run in perpendicular lines through the head. In small churches, windows of two or three lights are common, but in larger four or five lights for the aisles and clerestory windows, five or six for transepts and the end of aisles, and in the east and west windows seven, eight, and even nine lights, are used. Nine lights seem to be the extent, but there may be windows of this style containing more. The west window of York, and the east window of Lincoln cathedrals, are of eight lights each; the west window of Exeter cathedral, and the east window of Carlisle cathedral, are of nine, and these are nearly, if not quite, the largest windows remaining.

There may be observed two descriptions of tracery, and although, in different parts, they may have been worked at the same time, yet the first is generally the oldest. In this first division, the figures, such as circles, trefoils, quatrefoils, &c. are all worked with the same moulding, and do not always regularly join each other, but touch only at points. This may be called geometrical tracery; of this description are the windows of the nave of York, the eastern choir of Lincoln, and some of the tracery in the cloisters at Westminster abbey, as well as most of the windows at Exeter.

The second division consists of what may be truly called *flowing* tracery. Of this description, York minster, the minster and St. Mary's, at Beverley, Newark church, and many northern churches, as well as some southern churches, contain most beautiful specimens. The great west window at York, and the east window at Carlisle, are perhaps the most elaborate. In the richer windows of this style, and in both divisions, the principal moulding of the mullion has sometimes a capital and base, and thus becomes a shaft. One great cause of the beauty of fine flowing tracery, is the intricacy and delicacy of the mouldings; the principal moulding often running up only one or two mullions, and forming only a part of the larger design, and all the small figures being formed in mouldings which spring from the sides of the principal. The architraves of windows of this style are much ornamented with mouldings, which are sometimes made into shafts. The dripstones and canopies of windows are the same as in the doors, and have been described under that head. Wherever windows of this style remain, an artist should copy them; the varieties are much greater than might be supposed, for it is very difficult to find two alike in different buildings.

It does not appear that the straight horizontal transom was much if at all used in windows of this style; wherever it is found there is generally some mark of the window originating after the introduction of the Perpendicular style; but it may have been used in some places, and there are a very few instances of a light being divided in height by a kind of canopy or a quatrefoil breaking the mullion; the church of Dorchester, in Oxfordshire, has some very curious windows of this kind. In some counties, where flint and chalk are used, the dripstone is sometimes omitted. The heads of the windows of this style are most commonly the equilateral arch; though there are many examples both of lancet and drop arches; but the lancet arches are not very sharp. There are a few windows of this style with square heads; but they are not very common.

The circular windows of this style are some of them very fine; there are several very good ones in composition at Exeter and Chichester, and the east window of old St. Paul's was a very fine one; but perhaps the richest remaining is that at the south transept at Lincoln, which is completely flowing.

Towards the end of this style, and perhaps after the commencement of the next, we find windows of most beautiful composition, with parts like the Perpendicular windows, and sometimes a building has one end Decorated, the other Perpendicular; such is Melrose abbey, whose windows have been extremely fine, and indeed the great east window of York, which is the finest Perpendicular window in England, has still some traces of flowing lines in its head.

This window has also its architrave full of shafts and mouldings, which kind of architrave for windows is seldom continued far into the Perpendicular style; and therefore when a Perpendicular window has its architraves so filled with mouldings, it may be considered early in the style.

DECORATED ENGLISH ARCHES.

Though the arch most commonly used for general purposes in this style is the equilateral one, yet this is by no means constant. At York this arch is used, but at Ely a drop arch. The architrave mouldings of interior arches do not differ much from those of the last style, except that they are, perhaps, more frequently continued down the pier without being stopt at the line of capitals, and that the mouldings composing them are of larger size and bolder character, though in large buildings still consisting of many mouldings; of this, one of the finest examples is the architrave of the choir-arches at Litchfield, which is one of the best specimens of the different combinations of mouldings in this style. The distinction between the Early English small multiplied mouldings and the bold Decorated ones, may be well observed at Chester, where the arch between the choir and lady-chapel is very good Early English, and the arches of the nave as good Decorated work; and these two also show the difference of character of the two descriptions of pier.

The dripstones are of delicate mouldings, generally supported by heads. The arches of the galleries are often beautifully ornamented with foliated heads, and fine canopies; and in these arches the ogee arch is sometimes used, as it is freely in composition in the heads of windows.

Decorated English Piers.

A new disposition of shafts marks very decidedly
this style in large buildings, they being arranged
diamondwise, with straight sides, often containing as
many shafts as will stand close to each other at the
capital, and only a fillet or small hollow between
them. The shaft which runs up to support the roof,
often springs from a rich corbel between the outer
architrave mouldings of the arches; Exeter and Ely
are fine examples. The capitals and bases of these
shafts are much the same as those described in the
section on doors. Another pier of the richest effect,
but seldom executed, is that at York minster, where
the centre shaft is larger than those on each side, and
the three all run through to the spring of the roof.
Three also support the side of the arch; these shafts
are larger in proportion than those of Exeter, &c. and
stand nearly close without any moulding between.

Another pier, common towards the end of this style,
and the beginning of the next, is composed of four
shafts, about two-fifths engaged, and a fillet and bold
hollow half as large as the shafts between each; this
makes a very light and beautiful pier, and is much
used in small churches. All these kinds of piers
have their shafts sometimes filleted, and the architrave
mouldings are often large ogees. In small country
churches, the multangular flat-faced pier seems to have
been used.

Decorated English Buttresses.

These, though very various, are all more or less
worked in stages, and the set-offs variously ornamented,
some plain, some moulded slopes, some with triangular
heads, and some with pannels; some with niches in
them, and with all the various degrees of ornament.
The corner buttresses of this style are often set

diagonally. In some few instances small turrets are used as buttresses. The buttresses are variously finished; some slope under the cornice, some just through it; some run up through the battlement, and are finished with pinnacles of various kinds.

Of rich buttresses there are three examples which deserve great attention; the first is in the west front of York minster, and may be considered in itself as a magazine of the style; its lower part, to which it ascends without set-off, consists of four series of niches and pannelling of most delicate execution; above this part it rises as a buttress to the tower, in four stages of pannels, with triangular crocketed set-offs. The first of these stages contains a series of statuary niches, the rest are only pannelled. This buttress finishes under the cornice with an ornamented pannel and crocketed head; the projection of the lower part of this buttress is very great, and gives to the whole great boldness as well as richness. The second is a ruin, the east end of Howden church, Yorkshire; it has also some niches, but not so many as that at York. The third is also a ruin, the east end of the priory at Walsingham, in Norfolk; this is very late, and perhaps may be considered as almost a Perpendicular work, but it has so much of the rich magnificence of the Decorated style, that from its great plain spaces it deserves noticing as such; it is in fact a flat buttress set up against one face of an octagonal turret, and terminates in a fine triangular head richly crocketed. The buttress of the aisles of the nave of York minster are small compared with those at the west end, but their composition is singular, and of very fine effect; they run high above the parapet as a stay for the flying buttresses, and are finished by rich pinnacles.

Decorated English Tablets.

The cornice is very regular, and though in some
large buildings it has several mouldings, it principally
consists of a slope above, and a deep sunk hollow,
with an astragal under it ; in these hollows, flowers at
regular distances are often placed, and in some large
buildings, and in towers, &c. there are frequently
heads, and the cornice almost filled with them. The
dripstone is of the same description of mouldings, but
smaller, and this too is sometimes enriched with
flowers. The small tablet running under the window
has nearly the same mouldings, and this sometimes
runs round the buttress also. The dripstone very
seldom, if ever, runs horizontally, though in a few
instances a return is used instead of the more common
corbel head.

The general base tablet of this style is an ogee,
under which is a plain face, then a slope and another
plain face ; and it is not common to find real Decorated
buildings with more tablets, although both in the
Early English and Perpendicular styles, three, four,
and even five are sometimes used. And here another
singularity with respect to tablets may be mentioned ;
it is common in Early English work for the dripstone
to be carried horizontally after the return at the spring
of the arch, till stopt by a buttress, &c. and sometimes
it is even carried round the buttress :—and the same
arrangement is common in Perpendicular work, but
very rarely, if ever, is it so used in the Decorated style.

Decorated English Niches.

These form one of the greatest beauties of the style,
and are very various, but may be divided into two
grand divisions, which, if necessary, might be again
variously divided, such is their diversity, but these
two may be sufficient. The first are pannelled niches,

the fronts of whose canopies are even with the face of the wall or buttress they are set in. These have their interiors either square with a sloping side, or are regular semi-hexagons, &c. In the first case, if not very deep, the roof is a plain arch; but in the latter case, the roof is often most delicately groined, and sometimes a little shaft is set in the angles, or the ribs of the roof are supported by small corbels. The pedestals are often high and much ornamented.

The other division of niches have projecting canopies; these are of various shapes, some conical like a spire, some like several triangular canopies joined at the edges, and some with ogee heads; and in some very rich buildings are niches with the canopy bending forwards in a slight ogee, as well as its contour being an ogee; these are generally crowned with very large rich finials, and very highly enriched. There were also, at the latter part of this style, some instances of the niche with a flat-headed canopy, which became so common in the next style. These projecting niches have all some projecting base, either a large corbel, or a basement pedestal carried up from the next projecting face below. All these niches are occasionally flanked by small buttresses and pinnacles; those of the first kind have very often beautiful shafts.

The chancel stalls, of this style, are many of them uncommonly rich, their whole faces being often covered with ornamental carving.

Under this head, though not strictly niches, may be mentioned, what appears to be very rare, some wood carvings of a screen of this style; they consist of ten or more divisions of pannelling in the church of Lancaster; part form at present a screen for a vestry, &c. and part are in a gallery as a lining to the wall; their composition is alike and simple, being an arched head pannel with a triangular canopy between two buttresses crowned with pinnacles; they are, however, extremely rich, and varied in their details;

the buttresses are pannelled with diversified tracery, and the arch is an ogee canopy doubly feathered, and filled with tracery, as is the space between the ogee canopy and the triangular one, and both canopies are crocketed and crowned by rich finials; though they may be late in the style, yet the diversity of tracery and boldness of character, combined with simplicity of composition, so different from the elaborate and gorgeous screen-work of Perpendicular date, seem to mark them clearly as of the Decorated style.

DECORATED ENGLISH ORNAMENTS.

As the word Decorated is used to designate this style, and particularly as the next has been called florid, as if it were richer in ornament than this, it will be necessary to state, that though ornament is often profusely used in this style, yet these ornaments are like Grecian enrichments, and may be left out without destroying the grand design of the building, while the ornaments of the next are more often a minute division of parts of the building, as pannels, buttresses, &c. than the carved ornaments used in this style. In some of the more magnificent works, a variety of flowered carvings are used all over, and yet the building does not appear overloaded; while some of the late Perpendicular buildings have much less flowered carvings, yet look overloaded with ornaments, from the fatiguing recurrence of minute parts, which prevent the comprehension of the general design.

The flower of four leaves in a hollow moulding, has already been spoken of, and in these hollow mouldings various other flowers are introduced, as well as heads and figures, some of them very grotesque; and the capitals are very seldom found two alike. The foliage forming the crockets and finials is also extremely rich, and the pinnacle, in its various forms, is almost constantly used. The spandrels of ornamental arches are sometimes filled with beautiful foliage.

G

An ornament almost as peculiar to the Decorated style as the toothed ornament to the Early English, is a small round bud of three or four leaves, which open just enough to show a ball in the centre; this is generally placed in a hollow moulding, and has a beautiful effect. On the steeple of Salisbury, knobs are used very profusely in many parts as crockets; these are plain, but are so most likely on account of the distance from the eye; these and some other details show the Decorated date of this steeple, though its composition is assimilated to the Early English building it is raised upon. It is seldom safe to judge of date solely by the character of the ornamental carvings, yet in many instances these will be very clear distinctions. It is extremely difficult to describe, in words, the different characters of Early English and Decorated foliage, yet any one who attentively examines a few examples of each style, will seldom afterwards be mistaken, unless in buildings so completely transitional as to have almost every mark of both styles. There is in the Early English a certain unnatural character in the foliage, which is extremely stiff, when compared with the graceful and easy combinations, and the natural appearance of most of the well-executed Decorated foliage; in no place can this be examined with better effect than at the cathedrals of York and Ely, both of which contain very excellent examples of each style.

Decorated English Steeples.

At the commencement of this style, several fine spires were added to towers then existing, and in after times many very fine towers and spires were erected. Grantham, Newark, and several other Lincolnshire spires are very fine. These are generally flanked with buttresses, many of which are diagonal, and are generally crowned with fine pinnacles. Of these spires, Newark deserves peculiar attention, it rises engaged in the west end of the church, and the lower parts are Early English, but it is the upper story of the tower and the spire which are its principal beauties. This story rises from a band (which completely surrounds the tower) of sunk pannels. The story consists of a flat buttress of not much projection on each side, thus making eight round the tower; these are in three stages, the two lower plain, with small plain set-offs, the upper pannelled with an ogee head, and an ogee canopy, above which is a triangular head to the buttress richly crocketed, which finishes the buttress under the cornice. Between these buttresses are two beautiful two-light windows, with rich canopies on the dripstone, and a general canopy over both, crocketed and finishing in a rich finial; in the point of this canopy, between the heads of the windows, is a statue in a plain small niche, and on each side of the windows are other statues in niches with ogee crocketed canopies. The tracery of these windows is very good, and the architraves, both of windows and niches, are composed of shafts. The cornice is filled with flowers and other ornaments at small intervals, and from the corners rise short octagonal pedestals, on which are beautiful pinnacles finishing in statues for finials. The parapet is enriched with sunk quatrefoil pannels, and the spire has plain ribs and additional slopes on the alternate sides; there are four heights of windows in alternate faces, all, except the top row, richly crocketed. On the whole, perhaps there are no specimens superior in composition and execution, and few equal. There are many small towers and spires which appear to be Decorated; but there are so many of them altered, and with appearances so much like the next style, that they require more than common examination before they are pronounced absolutely Decorated; and there does not appear (as far as the author has been able to examine) any rich ornamented tower of large size remaining, that is a pure Decorated building. The west towers of York minster come the nearest to purity, though the tracery of the belfry windows and the battlements are decidedly Perpendicular.

DECORATED ENGLISH BATTLEMENTS.

A parapet continues frequently to be used in the Decorated style, but it is often pierced in various shapes, of which quatrefoils in circles or without that inclosure, are very common, but another not so common is more beautiful; this is a waved line, the spaces of which are trefoiled; it is well executed at the small church of St. Mary Magdalen, at Oxford. Pierced battlements are become very common; of these the nave of York presents a fine specimen; the battlement is an arch trefoiled or cinquefoiled, and the interval a quatrefoil in a circle, the whole covered with a running tablet which runs both horizontally and vertically. This round quatrefoil is sometimes exchanged for a square quatrefoil, as at Melrose abbey. The plain battlement most in use in this style is one with small intervals, and the capping moulding only horizontal; but there may be some battlement perhaps of this date with the capping running both vertically and horizontally. In some small works of this style a flower is occasionally used as a finish above the cornice, but it is by no means common.

DECORATED ENGLISH ROOFS.

The Decorated groined roof is an increase on the last style in the number of ribs; those of the simplest kind consisted of the longitudinal and crossing rib at the point of the arches, with the cross springers and pier rib, with also an intermediate rib between the cross springers and the pier rib and the wall arch; and these intermediate ribs increased in number, and adorned with small ribs forming stars and other figures by their intersections, give a variety to the groining almost equal to the tracery of windows. In this style, the rib mouldings are generally an ogee for the exterior, and hollows and rounds, with different fillets, towards the ceiling; in some few instances a principal and secondary rib are employed. The bosses are placed at all the intersections, and are often most beautifully carved. Exeter cathedral is a fine example of the plain roof, and the nave of York of the richer description, as is also the chapter-house of York.

There are buildings in which, though the upper roof is shown, there is a preparation for an inner roof; such is Chester cathedral, where only the lady-chapel, and the aisles of the choir, are groined, and the whole of the rest of the church is open; but on the top of the shafts is the commencement springing of a stone roof. There is a chapel in a church in Cambridgeshire, Willingham, between Ely and Cambridge, which has a very singular roof; stone ribs rise like the timber ones, the intervals are pierced, and the slope of the roof is of stone; it is high pitched, and the whole appears of Decorated character.

There remain a few roofs, which appear to be of Decorated character, that are open to the roof framing, and have a sort of pannelled work in ogee quatrefoils in timber, between the principals, which have arched ornamental work; of this kind is the roof of Eltham palace. These are getting very scarce, as they are hardly ever repaired but by new work of a totally different kind.

DECORATED ENGLISH FRONTS.

The east fronts of Decorated buildings consist so often of one large window for the chancel or choir, and two smaller ones for the aisles, if there be any, that little need be said of their composition, as all its variation in general depends on the variety of buttresses, &c. used as finishings. Of these it may be sufficient to mention three, the east ends of Lincoln and Carlisle cathedrals, and Howden church. The first consists of a centre, and side aisles divided, and flanked by tall buttresses without set-offs, but pannelled, with canopy heads and small corbels, the angles finished with shafts, and the tops of the buttresses with a triangular crocketed head; under the windows, along the whole front, runs a line of pannels divided by small shafts, and above them a tablet. The great centre window has been described before; it has eight lights, has over it one of five lights, flanked by arch-headed pannels, and the gable has an ornamented crocketed capping, and a cross; behind the buttresses rise octagonal pinnacles with rich finials: the windows of the aisles are of three lights, and over them the gables are filled with three tier of pannels and a circle, plain capping, and a cross at the point. This front has a very fine effect, and is almost the only east front of a cathedral which can be seen at a proper distance. The east end of Carlisle is evidently a Decorated wall added to an Early English building; its aisles are different from each other, but all the buttresses are rich; its great beauty is the east window, which is of nine lights, and in the composition of the tracery is superior even to the west window of York, to which the centre mullion gives a stiffness not visible at Carlisle. At Howden, the tracery of the great window is destroyed, and the whole in ruins; but enough remains to show the symmetry of the composition, and the richness and delicacy of the execution.

The east end of Litchfield cathedral is a semi-hexagon, with very fine long windows of rich tracery; this is late in the style, and seems to have been much repaired at a still later date. Of west fronts one only need be mentioned, but that must be allowed to be nearly, if not quite, the finest west front in the kingdom; it is that of York; its towers and buttresses have already been spoken of, and it only remains to say, that the three doors are the finest specimens of Decorated doors in the kingdom; its great window is only excelled by that of Carlisle. The central part over the window finishes by a horizontal cornice and battlement, above which rises the pierced canopy of the window, and at some distance behind the gable of the roof rises with a front of fine tracery, and a pierced battlement. It is to be regretted, that this beautiful front is surrounded by buildings so near, that no good view can be obtained of it, as, from the eye being brought too near, the fine elevation of the towers is almost lost. Of smaller churches, the east end of Trinity church, Hull, deserves attention; the windows are very fine, but the centre one has a trace of Perpendicular work in it.

DECORATED ENGLISH PORCHES.

There are not many of these remaining, but under this head should be noticed three beautiful gates, which are in some degree assimilated to porches; these are the gates of the abbey at Bury St. Edmund's, of Thornton abbey in Lincolnshire, and of Augustine's monastery at Canterbury; they have all rich and beautifully ornamented gateways, with rooms over them, and their fronts ornamented with niches, windows, &c. and at St. Augustine's, two fine octagonal towers rise above the roof. These three are of very varied composition, but all contain very valuable details.

The general appearance of Decorated buildings is at once simple and magnificent; simple from the small number of parts, and magnificent from the size of the windows, and easy flow of the lines of tracery. In the interior of large buildings we find great breadth, and an enlargement of the clerestory windows, with a corresponding diminution of the triforium, which is now rather a part of the clerestory opening than a distinct member of the division. The roofing, from the increased richness of the groining, becomes an object of attention.

Though we have not the advantage of any one large building of this style in its pure state, like Salisbury in the last style, yet we have, besides many detached parts, the advantage of four most beautiful models, which are in the highest preservation. These are at Lincoln, Exeter, York, and Ely; and though differently worked, are all of excellent execution. Of these, Exeter and York are far the largest, and York, from the uncommon grandeur and simplicity of the design, is certainly the finest; ornament is no-where spared, yet there is a simplicity which is peculiarly pleasing. Lincoln has already been spoken of as assimilated to the Early English work around it; and Ely has, from the same necessity of assimilation to former work, a larger triforium arrangement than common; though not so bold in its composition as the nave of York, the work at Ely is highly valuable for the beauty and delicacy of its details. Amongst the many smaller churches, Trinity church, at Hull, deserves peculiar notice, as its Decorated part is of a character which could better than any be imitated in modern work, from the great height of its piers, and the smallness of their size. The remains of Melrose abbey are extremely rich, and though in ruins, its parts are yet very distinguishable. In imitations of this style, great delicacy is required to prevent its running into the next, which, from its straight perpendicular and horizontal lines, is so much easier worked; whatever ornaments are used, should be very cleanly executed, and highly finished.

Though not so numerous as the Norman or Perpendicular fonts, yet there are many good fonts of this style remaining, and at Luton in Bedfordshire, is erected round the font a beautiful chapel or baptistery, of very fine composition.

As an example of transition from this style to the next, the choir of York may be cited; the piers and arches retain the same form as in the Decorated work in the nave, but the windows, the screens, and above all, the east end, are clearly Perpendicular, and of very excellent character and execution. The windows still retain shafts and mouldings in the architraves, and the east window has a band of statuary niches as part of its architrave.

There are many fine castellated remains of this style; of these, it may be enough to mention Caernarvon castle, and the noble gateway to Lancaster castle.

Of the Fourth, or Perpendicular Style.

PERPENDICULAR ENGLISH DOORS.

The great distinction of Perpendicular doors from those of the last style, is the almost constant square head over the arch, which is surrounded by the outer moulding of the architrave, and the spandrel filled with some ornament, and over all a dripstone is generally placed. This ornamented spandrel in a square head, occurs in the porch to Westminster hall, one of the earliest Perpendicular buildings, and is continued to the latest period of good execution, and in a rough way much later. In large, very rich doors, a canopy is sometimes included in this square head, and sometimes niches are added at the sides, as at King's college chapel, Cambridge. This square head is not always used interiorly, for an ogee canopy is sometimes used, or pannels down to the arch, as at St. George's, Windsor; and there are some small exterior doors without the square head. The shafts used in these doors are small, and have mostly plain capitals, which are often octagonal, and the bases made so below the first astragal. But there are still, in the early part of the style, some flowered capitals; and in those to the shafts of piers, in small churches, it is common for the capital to have in its hollow one or two square flowers. The mouldings of the capitals often contain (more particularly in the later dates of the style) a member which is precisely the cyma-recta of Grecian work. In small works, the bases of shafts have many mouldings, repetitions of ogees are mostly used, intermixed with hollows or straight slopes. The architraves of these doors have generally one or more large hollows, sometimes filled with statuary niches, but more often plain; this large hollow, in the architraves of both doors and windows, is one of the best marks of this style.

PERPENDICULAR ENGLISH WINDOWS.

These are easily distinguished by their mullions running in perpendicular lines, and the transoms, which are now general. The varieties of the last style were in the disposition of the principal lines of the tracery; in this, they are rather in the disposition of the minute parts; a window of four or more lights is generally divided into two or three parts, by strong mullions running quite up, and the portion of arch between them doubled from the centre of the side division. In large windows, the centre one is again sometimes made an arch, and often in windows of seven or nine lights, the arches spring across, making two of four or five lights, and the centre belonging to each. The heads of windows, instead of being filled with flowing ramifications, have slender mullions running from the heads of the lights, between each principal mullion, and these have small transoms till the window is divided into a series of small pannels; and the heads being arched, are trefoiled or cinquefoiled. Sometimes these small mullions are crossed over each other in small arches, leaving minute quatrefoils, and these are carried across in straight lines. Under the transom is generally an arch; but in Yorkshire, Lincolnshire, and Nottinghamshire, and perhaps in some other parts, there is a different mode of foliating the straight line without an arch, which has a singular appearance. In the later windows of this style, the transoms are often ornamented with small battlements, and sometimes with flowers, which, when well executed, have a very fine effect. Amidst so great a variety of windows, (for perhaps full half the windows in English edifices over the kingdom are of this style,) it is difficult to particularize; but St. George's, Windsor, for four lights, and the clerestory windows of Henry the VII.'s chapel for five, are some of the best executed. For a large window, the east window of York has no equal, and by taking its parts, a window of any size may be formed. There are some good windows, of which the heads have the mullions alternate, that is, the perpendicular line rises from the top of the arch of the pannel below it. The windows of the Abbey-church, at Bath, are of this description. The east window of the Beauchamp chapel at Warwick, is extremely rich, and has both within and without many singularities. The mullions which divide it into three parts, have a part of the great hollow for their moulding, which on the inside is filled with very rich statuary niches; the centre part of this window is divided into very minute pannellings in the upper part.

It is necessary here to say a little of a window which may be mistaken for a Decorated window; this is one of three lights, used in many country churches; the mullions simply cross each other, and are cinque-foiled in the heads, and quatrefoiled in the three upper spaces; but to distinguish this from a Decorated window, it will generally be necessary to examine its arch, its mullion mouldings, and its dripstone, as well as its being (as it often is) accompanied by a clearly Perpendicular window at the end, or connected with it so as to be evidently of that time. Its arch is very often four-centred, which at once decides its date; its mullion mouldings are often small, and very delicately worked; its dripstone in many instances has some clear mark.

and when the Decorated tracery is become familiar, it
will be distinguished from it by its being a mere folia-
tion of a space, and not a flowing quatrefoil with the
mouldings carried round it.

Large circular windows do not appear to have been
in use in this style; but the tracery of the circles in
the transepts of Westminster abbey appear to have
been renewed during this period. At Henry the VII.'s
chapel, a window is used in the aisles which seems to
have led the way to that wretched substitute for fine
tracery, the square-headed windows of queen Elizabeth and king James the first's time. This window is
a series of small pannels forming a square head, and it
is not flat but in projections, and these, with the
octagonal towers used for buttresses, throw the exterior
of the building into fritter, ill-assorting with the boldness of the clerestory windows. In most of the later
buildings of this style, the window and its architrave
completely fill up the space between the buttresses,
and the east and west windows are often very large;
the west window of St. George's, Windsor, has fifteen
lights in three divisions, and is a grand series of
pannels, from the floor to the roof; the door is amongst
the lower ones, and all above the next to the door is
pierced for the window. The east window at Gloucester is also very large, but that is of three distinct
parts, not in the same line of plan.

When canopies are used, which is not so often as
in the last style, they are generally of the ogee
character, beautifully crocketed.

PERPENDICULAR ENGLISH ARCHES.

Although the four-centred arch is much used,
particularly in the latter part of the style, yet, as in
all the other styles, we have in this also arches of
almost all sorts amongst the ornamental parts of niches,
&c. and in the composition lines of pannels, are arches
from a very fine thin lancet to an almost flat segment.

Yet, with all this variety, the four-centred arch is the one most used in large buildings, and the arches of other character, used in the division of the aisles, begin to have what is one of the great distinctions of this style,—the almost constant use of mouldings running from the base all round the arch, without any stop horizontally, by way of capital; sometimes with one shaft and capital, and the rest of the lines running; the shafts in front running up without stop to the roof, and from their capitals springing the groins. In window arches, shafts are now very seldom used, the architrave running all round, and both window arches and the arches of the interior, are often inclosed in squares, with ornamented spandrels, either like the doors, or of pannelling. Interior arches have seldom any dripstone when the square is used.

Another great distinction of these arches, in large buildings, is the absence of the triforium or gallery, between the arches of the nave and the clerestory windows; their place is now supplied by pannels, as at St. George's, Windsor, or statuary niches, as at Henry the VII.'s chapel; or they are entirely removed, as at Bath, and Manchester Old church, &c.

PERPENDICULAR ENGLISH PIERS.

The massive Norman round pier, lessened in size and extended in length, with shafts set round it, became the Early English pier; the shafts were multiplied, and set into the face of the pier, which became, in its plan, lozenge, and formed the Decorated pier. We now find the pier again altering in shape, becoming much thinner between the arches, and its proportion the other way, from the nave to the aisle, increased, by having those shafts which run to the roof, to support the springings of the groins, added in front, and not forming a part of the mouldings of the arch, but having a bold hollow between them: this is particularly apparent at King's college chapel, Cambridge, St.

George's, Windsor, and Henry the VII.'s chapel, the three great models of enriched Perpendicular style; but it is observable in a less degree in many others. In small churches, the pier mentioned in the last style, of four shafts and four hollows, is still much used; but many small churches have humble imitations of the magnificent arrangement of shafts and mouldings spoken of above. There are still some plain octagonal, &c. piers, in small churches, which may belong to this age.

Though filleted shafts are not so much used as in the last style, the exterior moulding of the architrave of interior arches is sometimes a filleted round, which has a good effect; and in general the mouldings and parts of piers, architraves, &c. are much smaller than those used in the last style, except the large hollows before mentioned.

PERPENDICULAR ENGLISH BUTTRESSES.

These differ very little from those of the last style, except that triangular heads to the stages are much less used, the set-offs being much more often bold projections of plain slopes; yet many fine buildings have the triangular heads. In the upper story, the buttresses are often very thin, and have diagonal faces. There are few large buildings of this style without flying buttresses, and these are often pierced; at Henry the VII.'s chapel they are of rich tracery, and the buttresses are octagonal turrets. At King's college chapel, Cambridge, which has only one height within, the projection of the buttresses is so great as to allow chapels between the wall of the nave, and another level with the front of the buttresses. At Gloucester, and perhaps at some other places, an arch or half arch is pierced in the lower part of the buttress. There are a few buildings of this style without any buttresses. All the kinds are occasionally ornamented with statuary niches, and canopies of various descriptions, and the diagonal corner buttress is not so common as in the last style; but the two buttresses often leave a square, which runs up, and sometimes, as at the tower of the Old church at Manchester, is crowned with a third pinnacle.

Although pinnacles are used very freely in this style, yet there are some buildings, whose buttresses run up and finish square without any; of this description is St. George's, Windsor, and the Beauchamp chapel. The buttresses of the small eastern addition at Peterborough cathedral are curious, having statues of saints for pinnacles.

In interior ornaments, the buttresses used are sometimes small octagons, sometimes pannelled, sometimes plain, and then, as well as the small buttresses of niches, are often banded with a band different from the Early English, and much broader. Such are the buttresses between the doors of Henry the VII.'s chapel.

The small buttresses of this style attached to screenwork, stall-work, and niches, are different from any before used, and they form a good mark of the style. The square pedestal of the pinnacle being set with an angle to the front, is continued down, and on each side is set a small buttress of a smaller face than this pedestal, thus leaving a small staff between them; these buttresses have set-offs, and this small staff at each set-off has the moulding to it, which being generally two long hollows, and a fillet between, has on the staff an appearance of a spear head. It is not easy to describe this buttress in words, but when once seen, it will be easily recognised; and as almost every screen and tabernacle niche is ornamented with them in this style, they need not be long sought. The niches in front of Westminster hall, (one of the best and earliest Perpendicular examples,) and the niches under the clerestory windows of Henry the VII.'s chapel, (one of the latest) have them almost exactly similar.

PERPENDICULAR ENGLISH TABLETS,

The cornice is now, in large buildings, often composed of several small mouldings, sometimes divided by one or two considerable hollows, not very deep; yet still, in plain buildings, the old cornice mouldings are much adhered to; but it is more often ornamented in the hollow with flowers, &c. and sometimes with grotesque animals; of this the churches of Gresford and Mold, in Flintshire, are curious examples, being a complete chase of cats, rats, mice, dogs, and a variety of imaginary figures, amongst which various grotesque monkeys are very conspicuous. In the latter end of the style, something very analogous to an ornamented frieze is perceived, of which the canopies to the niches, in various works, are examples; and the angels so profusely introduced, in the later rich works, are a sort of cornice ornaments. These are very conspicuous at St. George's, Windsor, and Henry the VII.'s chapel. At Bath, is a cornice of two hollows, and a round between with fillets, both upper and under surface nearly alike. The dripstone of this style is, in the heads of doors and some windows, much the same as in the last style, and it most generally finishes by a plain return; though corbels are sometimes used, this return is frequently continued horizontally.

Tablets under the windows are like the dripstone, and sometimes fine bands are carried round as tablets. Of these there are some fine remains at the cathedral, and at the tower of St. John's, Chester.

The basement mouldings ordinarily used are not materially different from the last style; reversed ogees and hollows, variously disposed, being the principal mouldings; but in rich buildings several mouldings and alternate faces are used.

Perpendicular English Niches.

These are very numerous, as amongst them we
must include nearly all the stall, tabernacle, and
screen-work in the English churches; for there appears
little wood-work of an older date, and it is probable
that much screen-work was defaced at the Reformation,
but restored in queen Mary's time, and not again
destroyed; at least the execution of much of it would
lead to such a supposition, being very full of minute
tracery, and much attempt at stiffly ornamented
friezes. The remains of oak screen-work and tracery
are much greater than would be conceived possible,
considering the varied destructions of the Reformation
and civil war. Most of our cathedrals, and very many
smaller churches, contain tabernacle and screen-work
in excellent condition, and of beautiful execution; and
amongst this kind of work should be reckoned the
great number of stalls with turn-up seats and benches;
these, though many of them are of abominable composition, are by no means all so; the ceremonies of
the church, legends, and above all, figures of animals,
flowers, and foliage, admirably designed and executed, make up by far the greater number. At St.
Michael's church, Coventry, are many of the best character. The benches before these stalls present, in their
ends and fronts, combinations of pannelling and flower-
work of great beauty. As an instance how late
wood-work was executed in a good style, there is some
screen-work in the church at Huyton in Lancashire,
in which the date is cut in such a way as to preclude
any doubt of its being done at the time; and the date
is corroborated by armorial bearings carved on the
same work; this date is 1663, a time at which all idea of
executing good English work in stone seems to have
been lost. Many niches are simple recesses, with rich
ogee canopies, and others have over-hanging square-

H

headed canopies, with many minute buttresses and pinnacles, crowned with battlements; or, in the latter part of the style, with what has been called the Tudor flower, an ornament used instead of battlement, as an upper finish, and profusely strewed over the roofs, &c. of rich late buildings. Of these niches, those in Henry the VII.'s chapel, between the arches and clerestory windows, are perhaps as good a specimen as any. Of the plain recesses, with ogee canopies, there are some fine ones at Windsor.

The whole interior of the richer buildings of this style, is more or less a series of pannels; and therefore, as every pannel may, on occasion, become a niche, we find great variety of shape and size; but like those of the last style, they may generally be reduced to one or other of these divisions.

PERPENDICULAR ENGLISH ORNAMENTS.

The grand source of ornament, in this style, is pannelling; indeed, the interior of most rich buildings is only a general series of it; for example, King's college chapel, Cambridge, is all pannel, except the floor; for the doors and windows are nothing but pierced pannels, included in the general design, and the very roof is a series of them of different shapes. The same may be said of the interior of St. George's, Windsor; and still further, Henry the VII.'s chapel is so both within and without, there being no plain wall all over the chapel, except the exterior from below the base moulding, all above is ornamental pannel. All the small chapels of late erection in this style, such as those at Winchester, and several at Windsor, are thus all pierced pannel. Exclusive of this general source of ornament, there are a few peculiar to it; one, the battlement to transoms of windows, has already been mentioned; this, in works of late date, is very frequent, sometimes extending to small transoms in the head of the window, as well as the general division of the lights. Another, the Tudor flower, is, in rich work, equally common, and forms a most beautiful enriched battlement, and is also sometimes used on the transoms of windows in small work. Another peculiar ornament of this style, is the angel cornice, used at Windsor and in Henry the VII.'s chapel; but though according with the character of those buildings, it is by no means fit for general use. These angels have been much diffused, as supporters of shields, and as corbels to support roof-beams, &c. Plain as the Abbey-church at Bath is in its general execution, it has a variety of angels as corbels, for different purposes.

A great number of edifices of this style appear to have been executed in the reign of Henry the VII, as the angels so profusely introduced into his own works, and also his badges — the rose and portcullis, and sometimes his more rare cognizances, are abundantly scattered in buildings of this style.

Flowers of various kinds continue to ornament cornices, &c. and crockets were variously formed towards the end of the style, those of pinnacles were often very much projected, which has a disagreeable effect; there are many of these pinnacles at Oxford, principally worked in the decline of the style.

Perpendicular English Steeples.

Of these there remain specimens of almost every description, from the plain short tower of a country church, to the elaborate and gorgeous towers of Gloucester and Wrexham. There are various fine spires of this style, which have little distinction from those of the last, but their age may be generally known by their ornaments, or the towers supporting them. Almost every conceivable variation of buttress, battlement, and pinnacle, is used, and the appearance of many of the towers combines, in a very eminent degree, extraordinary richness of execution and grandeur of design. Few counties in England are without some good examples; besides the two already mentioned, Boston in Lincolnshire, All Saints in Derby, St. Mary's at Taunton, St. George's, Doncaster, are celebrated; and the plain, but excellently proportioned, tower of Magdalen college, Oxford, deserves much attention.

Amongst the smaller churches, there are many towers of uncommon beauty, but few exceed Gresford, between Chester and Wrexham; indeed, the whole of this church, both interior and exterior, is worth attentive examination. Paunton, near Grantham, has also a tower curious for its excellent masonry. There are of this style some small churches with fine octagonal lanterns, of which description are two in the city of York; and of this style is that most beautiful composition, the steeple of St. Nicholas, at Newcastle-upon-Tyne, — a piece of composition equally remarkable for its simplicity, delicacy, and excellent masonic arrangement. Early in this style also is the steeple of St. Michael at Coventry, which, but for the extreme destruction of its ornaments, in consequence of the nature of the stone, would be nearly unequalled. To notice all the magnificent towers of this style would take a volume, but the cathedrals at Canterbury and York must not be omitted. At Canterbury, the central tower, which has octagonal turrets at the corners, is a very fine one; and the south-west tower, which has buttresses and fine pinnacles, though in a different style, is little inferior. At York, the centre tower is a most magnificent lantern; its exterior looks rather flat, from its not having pinnacles, which seem to have been intended by the mode in which the buttresses are finished; but its interior gives, from the flood of light it pours into the nave and transepts, a brilliancy of appearance equalled by very few, if any, of the other cathedrals.

PERPENDICULAR ENGLISH BATTLEMENTS.

Parapets still continue to be used occasionally. The trefoiled pannel with serpentine line is still used, but the dividing line is oftener straight, making the divisions regular triangles.

Of pannelled parapets, one of the finest is that of the Beauchamp chapel, which consists of quatrefoils in squares, with shields and flowers.

Of pierced battlements there are many varieties, but the early ones frequently have quatrefoils, either for the lower compartments, or on the top of the pannels of the lower, to form the higher; the later have often two heights of pannels, one range for the lower, and another over them forming the upper; and at Loughborough is a fine battlement of rich pierced quatrefoils, in two heights, forming an indented battlement. These battlements have generally a running cap moulding carried round, and generally following the line of battlement. There are a few late buildings, which have pierced battlements, not with straight tops, but variously ornamented; such is the tomb-house at Windsor, with pointed upper compartments; and such is the battlement of the eastern addition at Peterborough, and the great battlement of King's college chapel, Cambridge, and also that most delicate battlement over the lower side chapels; this is perhaps the most elegant of the kind. Sometimes on the outside, and often within, the Tudor flower is used as a battlement, and there are a few instances of the use of a battlement analogous to it in small works long before; such is that at Waltham cross.

Of plain battlements there are many descriptions: 1st, that of nearly equal intervals, with a plain capping running round with the outline. 2nd, The castellated battlement, of nearly equal intervals, and sometimes with large battlements and small intervals, with the cap moulding running only horizontally, and the sides cut plain. 3d, A battlement like the last, with the addition of a moulding which runs round the outline, and has the horizontal capping set upon it. 4th, The most common late battlement, with the cap moulding broad, of several mouldings, and running round the outline, and thus often narrowing the intervals, and enlarging the battlement. To one or other of these varieties, most battlements may be reduced; but they are never to be depended on alone, in determining the age of a building, from the very frequent alterations they are liable to.

PERPENDICULAR ENGLISH ROOFS.

These may be divided into three kinds; first, those open to the roof framing; second, those ceiled flat or nearly so; and thirdly, the regular groined roof.

Of the first kind are those magnificent timber roofs, of which Westminster hall is one of the finest specimens. The beams, technically called *principals,* are here made into a sort of trefoil arch, and the interstices of the framing filled with pierced pannellings; there are also arches from one principal to another. Crosby hall in Bishopsgate-street, is another roof of this description, as is the hall of Christchurch, Oxford, and many others: this roof is not often found in churches.

The second is common in churches, and is the Perpendicular ordinary style of cieling, rich, though easily constructed; a rib crossed above the pier, with a small flat arch, and this was crossed by another in the centre of the nave, and the spaces thus formed were again divided by cross ribs, till reduced to squares of two or three feet; and at each intersection, a flower, shield, or other ornament was placed. This roof was sometimes in the aisles made sloping, and occasionally coved. In a few instances, the squares were filled with fans, &c. of small tracery. A variety of this roof which is very seldom met with, is a real flat cieling, like the ordinary domestic cieling of the present day; of this, the post room at Lambeth palace offers one specimen, and a room attached to St. Mary's hall, at Coventry, another; both these have small ribs crossing the cieling, and dividing it into several parts. At Coventry, the intersection of these ribs in the centre, and their spring from the moulding, which runs round from the side walls, are ornamented with carvings.

The third, or groined roof, is of several kinds. Of this it may be well to notice, that the ribs in this style are frequently of fewer mouldings than before, often only a fillet and two hollows, like a plain mullion. We see in the groined roofs of this style almost every possible variety of disposition of the ribs, and in the upper part of the arch they are in many instances feathered; and these ribs are increased in the later roofs, till the whole is one series of net-work, of which the roof of the choir, at Gloucester, is one of the most complicated specimens. The late monumental chapels, and statuary niches, mostly present in their roofs very complicated tracery.

We now come to a new and most delicate description of roof, that of *fan tracery,* of which probably the earliest, and certainly one of the most elegant, is that of the cloisters at Gloucester. In these roofs, from the top of the shaft springs a small fan of ribs, which doubling out from the points of the pannels, ramify on the roof, and a quarter or half-circular rib forms the fan, and the lozenge interval is formed by some of the ribs of the fan running through it, and dividing it into portions, which are filled with ornament. King's college chapel, Cambridge, Henry the VII.'s chapel, and the Abbey-church at Bath, are the best specimens, after the Gloucester cloisters; and to these may be added the aisles of St. George's, Windsor, and that of the eastern addition to Peterborough. To some of these roofs are attached pendants, which, in Henry the VII.'s chapel, and the Divinity school at Oxford, come down as low as the springing line of the fans.

The roof of the nave and choir of St. George's, Windsor, is very singular, and perhaps unique. The ordinary proportion of the arches and piers is half the breadth of the nave; this makes the roof compartments two squares, but at Windsor the breadth of the nave is nearly three times that of the aisles, and this makes a figure of about three squares. The two exterior parts are such as, if joined, would make a very rich, ribbed roof; and the central compartment, which runs as a flat arch, is filled with tracery pannels, of various shapes, ornamented with quatrefoils, and forming two halves of a star; in the choir, the centre of the star is a pendant. This roof is certainly the most singular, and perhaps the richest in effect of any we have; it is profusely adorned with bosses, shields, &c.

There still remains one more description of roof, which is used in small chapels, but not common in large buildings. This is the arch roof; in a few instances it is found plain, with a simple ornament at the spring and the point, and this is generally a moulding with flowers, &c. but it is mostly pannelled. Of this roof, the nave of the Abbey-church at Bath is a most beautiful specimen. The arch is very flat, and is composed of a series of small rich pannels, with a few large ones at the centre of the compartments formed by the piers. The roofs of the small chapels, on the north side of the Beauchamp chapel, at Warwick, are also good examples; and another beautiful roof of this kind is the porch to Henry the VII.'s chapel; but this is so hidden, from the want of light, as to be seldom noticed.

The ribbed roofs are often formed of timber and plaster, but are generally coloured to represent stone-work.

There may be some roofs of different arrangements from any of these; but in general they may be referred to one or other of the above heads.

PERPENDICULAR ENGLISH FRONTS.

The first to be noticed of these, and by far the finest west front, is that of Beverley minster, a building much less known than its great value merits it should be. What the west front of York is to the Decorated style, this is to the Perpendicular, with this addition, that in this front nothing but one style is seen,—all is harmonious. Like York minster, it consists of a very large west window to the nave, and two towers for the end of the aisles. This window is of nine lights, and the tower windows of three lights. The windows in the tower correspond in range nearly with those of the aisles and clerestory windows of the nave; the upper windows of the tower are belfry windows. Each tower has four large and eight small pinnacles, and a very beautiful battlement. The whole front is pannelled, and the buttresses, which have a very bold projection, are ornamented with various tiers of niche-work, of excellent composition and most delicate execution. The doors are uncommonly rich, and have the hanging feathered ornament; the canopy of the great centre door runs up above the sill of the window, and stands free in the centre light, with a very fine effect. The gable has a real tympanum, which is filled with fine tracery. The east front is fine, but mixed with Early English. The west fronts of Winchester, Gloucester, Chester, Bath, and Windsor, are all of this style, and all of nearly the same parts;—a great window and two side ones, with a large door and sometimes side ones; Chester has only one side window. Though in some respects much alike, they are really very different. Winchester has three rich porches to its doors; Gloucester a very rich battlement, with the canopy of the great window running through it; Chester a very fine door, with niches on each side; Bath, a curious representation of Jacob's dream, the ladders forming a sort of buttresses, and angels filling the space about the head of the great window ; Windsor is plain, except its noble window and beautiful pierced parapet and battlements: but it is curious that in all these examples the nave is flanked by octagonal towers; at Winchester and Gloucester, crowned with pinnacles; at Chester and Windsor with ogee heads, and at Bath by an open battlement. The ends of King's college chapel, Cambridge, are nearly alike, but that one has a door and the other not; these also are flanked with octagonal towers, which are finished with buttresses, pinnacles, and an ogee top. Of east ends, York is almost the only one which preserves the whole elevation, and this is the richest of all; it is highly ornamented with niches in the buttresses, and has octagonal turrets which finish in very tall pinnacles, of a size equal to small spires, but which, from the great elevation of the front, do not appear at all too large. Of small churches, the west end of St. George, Doncaster, and Trinity church, Hull, are fine examples ; as are the east ends of Louth church in Lincolnshire, and Warwick church, as well as its beautiful companion the Beauchamp chapel.

Perpendicular English Porches.

Of these there are so many that it is no easy matter to chuse examples, but three may be noticed ; first, that attached to the south-west tower of Canterbury cathedral, which is covered with fine niches ; secondly, the south porch at Gloucester, which has more variety of outline, and is nearly as rich in niches ; the third is the north porch at Beverley, and this is, as a pannelled front, perhaps unequalled. The door has a double canopy, the inner an ogee, and the outer a triangle, with beautiful crockets and tracery, and is flanked by fine buttresses breaking into niches, and the space above the canopy to the cornice, is pannelled ; the battlement is composed of rich niches, and the buttresses crowned by a group of four pinnacles. The

small porches of this style are many of them very
fine, but few equal those of King's college chapel,
Cambridge.

The appearance of Perpendicular buildings is very
various, so much depends on the length to which
pannelling, the great source of ornament, is carried.
The triforium is almost entirely lost, the clerestory
windows resting often on a string which bounds the
ornaments in the spandrels of the arches, but there is
not unfrequently under these windows, in large buildings, a band of sunk or pierced pannelling of great
richness.

Of this style so many buildings are in the finest
preservation, that it is difficult to select; but, on
various accounts, several claim particular mention.
The choir at York is one of the earliest buildings;
indeed it is, in general arrangements, like the nave,
but its ornamental parts, the gallery under the windows, the windows themselves, and much of its
pannelling in the interior, are completely of Perpendicular character, though the simple grandeur of the
piers is the same as the nave. The choir of Gloucester
is also of this style, and most completely so, for the
whole interior is one series of open-work pannels laid
on the Norman work, parts of which are cut away to
receive them; it forms a very ornamental whole, but
by no means a model for imitation.

Of the later character, are three most beautiful
specimens, King s college chapel, Cambridge, Henry
the VII.'s chapel, and St. George's, Windsor; in
these, richness of ornament is lavished on every part,
and they are particularly valuable for being extremely
different from each other, though in many respects
alike. Of these, undoubtedly St. George's, Windsor,
is the most valuable, from the great variety of composition arising from its plan ; but the roof and single
line of wall of King's college chapel, Cambridge,
deserves great attention, and the details of Henry the

VII.'s chapel will always command it, from the great delicacy of their execution.

Of small churches, there are many excellent models for imitation, so that in this style, with some care and examination, scarcely any thing need be executed but from absolute authority. The monumental chapels of this style are peculiarly deserving attention, and often of the most elaborate workmanship

The fonts of this style are very numerous, and of all sorts of workmanship, from the roughest description, to that most elaborate specimen at Walsingham church in Norfolk. To some of these remain font covers of wood, of which a few are composed of very good tabernacle-work.

The castellated remains of this style are generally much altered, to render them habitable; parts of Windsor castle are good; the exterior of Tattershall castle, in Lincolnshire, remains nearly unaltered.

Miscellaneous Remarks on Buildings of English Architecture.

Having now given an outline of the details of the different styles, it remains to speak of a few matters which could not so well be previously noticed. As one style passed gradually into another, there will be here and there buildings partaking of two, and there are many buildings of this description whose dates are not at all authenticated.

There is one building which deserves especial mention, from the singularity of its character, ornaments, and plan; this is Roslyn chapel. It is certainly unclassable as a whole, being unlike any other building in Great Britain of its age, (the latter part of the fifteenth century,) but if its details are minutely examined, they will be found to accord most completely, in the ornamental work, with the style then prevalent, though debased by the clumsiness of the parts, and their want of proportion to each other. There seems little doubt that the designer was a foreigner, or at least took some foreign buildings for his model.

It will be proper to add a few words on the alterations and additions which most ecclesiastical edifices have received; and some practical remarks as to judging of their age. The general alteration is that of windows, which is very frequent; very few churches are without some Perpendicular windows. We may therefore pretty safely conclude that a building is as old as its windows, or at least that part is so which contains the windows; but we can by no means say so with respect to doors, which are often left much older than the rest of the building.

A locality of style may be observed in almost every county, and in the districts where flint abounds, it is sometimes almost impossible to determine the date of the churches, from the absence of battlements, architraves, and buttresses; but wherever stone is used, it is seldom difficult to assign each part to its proper style, and with due regard to do the same with plates of ordinary correctness, a little habitual attention would enable most persons to judge at once, at the sight of a plate or drawing, of its correctness, from its consistency, or the contrary, with the details of its apparent style.

In a sketch like the present, it is impossible to notice every variety; but at least the author now presents the world with a rational arrangement of the details of a mode of architecture on many accounts valuable, and certainly the most proper for ecclesiastical edifices. Still further to enable the reader to distinguish the principles of Grecian and English architecture, he adds a few striking contrasts, which are formed by those principles in buildings of real purity, and which will at once convince any unprejudiced mind of the impossibility of any thing like a good mixture.

GRECIAN.

The general running lines are horizontal.

Arches not necessary.

An entablature absolutely necessary, consisting always of two, and mostly of three distinct parts, having a close relation to, and its character and ornaments determined by the columns.

The columns can support nothing but an entablature, and no arch can spring directly from a column.

A flat column may be called a pilaster, which can be used as a column.

The arch must spring from a horizontal line.

Columns the supporters of the entablature.

ENGLISH.

The general running lines are vertical.

Arches a really fundamental principal, and no pure English building or ornament can be composed without them.

No such thing as an entablature composed of parts, and what is called a cornice, bears no real relation to the shafts which may be in the same building.

The shafts can only support an arched moulding, and in no case a horizontal line.

Nothing analogous to a pilaster; every flat ornamented projecting surface, is either a series of pannels, or a buttress.

No horizontal line necessary, and never any but the small cap of a shaft.

Shaft bears nothing, and is only ornamental, and the round pier still a pier.

GRECIAN.	ENGLISH.
No projections like buttresses, and all projections stopped by horizontal lines.	Buttresses essential parts, and stop horizontal lines.
Arrangement of pediment fixed.	Pediment only an ornamented end wall, and may be of almost any pitch.
Openings limited by the proportions of the column.	Openings almost unlimited.
Regularity of composition on each side of a centre necessary.	Regularity of composition seldom found, and variety of ornament universal.
Cannot form good steeples, because they must resemble unconnected buildings piled on each other.	From its vertical lines, may be carried to any practicable height, with almost increasing beauty.

In the foregoing details we have said little of castel lated or domestic architecture; because there does not appear to be any remains of domestic buildings, so old as the latest period of the English style, which are unaltered; and because the castellated remains are so uncertain in their dates, and so much dilapidated or altered, to adapt them to modern modes of life or defence, that little clear arrangement could be made, and a careful study of ecclesiastical architecture will lead any one, desirous to form some judgment of the character of these buildings, to the most accurate conclusions on the subject which can well be obtained in their present state.

Nor has any thing been said of monuments, because, should they bear the name of the deceased, and the date of his death, they were often erected long after; thus Osric's tomb at Gloucester, and that of King John at Worcester, are both of Perpendicular date, if their style may be considered as any guide. Most of the monuments which are valuable, will have their style ascertained by what has been said of larger erections. There are many which deserve much attention, for the excellence of their workmanship and composition; of these may be noted those of Aymer de Valance, earl of Pembroke, in Westminster abbey, and a curious monument in Winchelsea church, Sussex; the monument of the Percys at Beverley; that of king Edward the II. at Gloucester, and that of Richard Beauchamp, earl of Warwick, in the centre of the Beauchamp chapel; with several at Canterbury, York, and Winchester.

There are two which are so singular, and so different from the style in use at the time of their erection, that they require particular remark; these are, the shrine of Edward the Confessor, and the tomb of Henry the III, both erected near the same time, and probably by the same artist, who has been stated to be an Italian; and this may account for the style of these monuments, where, with some few traces of the Early English, (the style in use at the time of their erection,) there is much close resemblance to Roman work; added to which they are covered with Mosaic work, which has been much used in Italy.

The object of this essay being to lead the student to examine and judge of buildings for himself, it has appeared advisable to refer him to some buildings in almost every part of the Kingdom; and in forming this list, (which follows the description of the plates,) it has been rather sought to refer to examples of good character than to swell the number by those which were doubtful; ruins have not often been referred to, except where they contain, either in composition or detail, some parts of considerable value; sometimes it is only a part of the building referred to which is valuable; and it should always be borne in mind, that the alterations which are continually taking place, may make some of the references incorrect. It is possible, that on the borders some churches may be placed in a wrong county, from the division not being well known.

Description of the Plates of English Architecture.

(No relative proportion has been preserved between the various subjects engraved on each plate, it being the forms which are to be considered, each of which is given of the size most convenient for the requisite clearness of delineation.)

PLATE V.

The design, in the centre of this plate, is intended to give a general view of various parts as usually defined; and no letters of reference are employed, that the student may the more completely acquire the knowledge of parts by mere description. It consists of a portion of wall, in which is a Perpendicular window of three lights and a transom. The transom heads of the lights are cinquefoiled in an ogee arch, and the upper lights in a plain arch; the secondary divisions above are trefoiled. This window has a dripstone with plain returns. There are three buttresses; two are square-set corner buttresses, (one seen in front and one in flank;) and one diagonal one, which is seen at its angle. These buttresses have each three stages, and three set-offs, and die under the cornice, which is flowered. The battlement is of equal intervals, and the capping runs only horizontally. Under the window is a tablet, which runs round the square buttresses, and stops against, or dies into, the diagonal one. The

I

base consists of two tablets; one an ogee and hollow, and the other a plain slope. This description ought to be so fully comprehended, that if measures were added, the student should be able to draw the design from the description, being furnished with sections, or some other mode of determining the mouldings.

The two uppermost lines of the plate contain various arches:

a, The semi-circular arch.   *b*, The segmental arch.

c, The equilateral arch.   *d*, The drop arch.

e, The lancet arch.   *f*, The horse-shoe arch.

g, The ogee arch.   *h*, The four-centred arch.

Then follow foliations or featherings:

i, A plain arch, trefoiled.

k, A square quatrefoil pannel, double feathered.

l, A square window-head, cinquefoiled.

m, A transom, with ogee-head to the light, cinquefoiled, and the spandrels trefoiled.

n, A trefoiled circle: this is of Early English character, and the points flowered.

o, A cinquefoiled circle.

p, Plan of a plain Norman pier.

q, A Norman pier with shafts.

r, An Early English pier with a centre.

s, An Early English pier from Salisbury.

t, A Decorated English pier from Chester.

u, A Decorated English pier from York.

w, *x*, Two Perpendicular English piers.

PLATE VI.

This plate contains parts of various styles.

a, The top of an ogee canopy, with plain bold crockets, and a finial which has under it a neck moulding.

b, A pinnacle, and part of its pedestal, which is pannelled, and has an ogee cinquefoiled head. The pinnacle has its canopies crocketed, with finials, and a plain neck moulding; the points stopt by figures.

The pinnacle has a finial and neck moulding, consisting of an astragal and two fillets.

c, The finishing of the buttresses of the Beauchamp chapel. The set-off seen is of bold hollows, and the pedestal rises with a two-light pannel with trefoiled heads. The upper part has four square pannels, which are quatrefoiled, and the plan made octagonal by figures at the corners supporting small shafts. In the capping, a flower is placed in the corners, and the whole has a small battlement.

d, A portion of a dripstone from York minster; it has the ball flower in the hollow, and two varieties of crockets.

e, A capping moulding, with two varieties of Early English crockets.

f, The common mullion moulding, used, with various proportions of its parts, in both the Decorated and Perpendicular styles.

g, A Perpendicular mullion of elaborate character, from the chancel of Warwick church.

h, Part of the same mullion with the exterior architrave.

i, Half of the principal mullions of the window at the west end of Beverley minster; this window contains four sets of mullions.

k, The common battlement capping, showing how it is finished at the back.

l, The common string moulding of Decorated and Perpendicular work, used for cornices and tablets of various descriptions, and of sizes according to its uses.

m, A beautiful tablet moulding, much used in rich Decorated buildings.

n, The most common late base moulding.

o, The Early English toothed ornament between two filleted rounds, its most usual position.

p, The square flower used in cornices, &c.; it is often made much richer than here represented.

q, A rose often used in late Perpendicular works, particularly in wood-work.

r, Plan of a division of groining; that is, a representation of its appearance looking up at it from under its centre. The ribs, which run from corner to corner, are called the cross springers, and the longer side line will be in this example the pier rib, and the shorter the arch rib on the wall; the short central line will be the longitudinal rib, (this being a division from a nave,) and the longer one the cross rib. In this example there is only one additional rib between the cross springers and the pier rib, and these are represented of smaller size. There are bosses at the intersections.

PLATE VII.

Plan of a cathedral, collegiate, or other church, in the form of a cross, with the usual additional buildings. It is not the plan of any particular building, but composed to introduce as many parts as it was expedient to describe. The cross lines represent the groinings of the roof, which, in plans of English buildings, are usually laid down on the principle of the division in the last plate.

a a, Towers at the west end.

b b, Porches.

c, The nave. *d d*, Side aisles of the nave.

e, The cloisters. *f*, The library.

g, The north transept.

h, The south transept.

i i, The side aisles of the south transept.

k k k, Chapels.

l, Chapter-house, with passage from the cloisters.

m, Central tower, cross, or lantern.

n, Screen, over which is usually placed the organ

o, Choir, at the east end of which is generally the altar.

p p, Side aisles of the choir.

q, Lady-chapel.

The small circles in several of the piers and walls, are staircases; the steps could not be shown on so small a scale. The organ screen, and inclosure of the choir, are of a lighter tint than the walls, to show that they are not continued to the top of the arches; against this inclosure are placed the stalls in a cathedral. The place of the bishop's throne varies, but it is generally on the south side, and the pulpit nearly opposite.

PLATE VIII.

Two steeples; one a Perpendicular tower with a lantern; this has octagonal turrets at the corners, with buttresses attached below; the lowest stages of the buttresses are pannelled. A band of quatrefoils runs under the belfry window, which is of three lights, and has a crocketed canopy; under the band of quatrefoils is a square-headed plain-arched cinquefoiled window. The dripstone of the door runs as a tablet round the buttresses. The base mouldings are of three tablets.

The other steeple in this plate is a Decorated tower and spire. The tower has diagonal buttresses of three stages, sloping to the wall, at some distance below the cornice, which is plain. The battlement has small intervals, and a horizontal capping. The spire is ribbed at the angles, and has four small windows with plain canopies. The belfry window is of two lights, set upon a plain string, which dies against the buttresses. Below is a small window without a dripstone, and at the bottom a larger one with a dripstone, and set on a string. The base mouldings have two tablets.

PLATE IX.

A Norman composition, which may be considered as a view of one side of a nave, flanked with a small tower, with two stages of ornamental arches, the lower intersecting, and a window above. The buttresses are plain; those below have a projection beyond the parapet, those above are without. The windows are various, and the door-way has shafts and several ornamented mouldings.

a, A string moulding, consisting of a fillet with the alternate billet moulding, and a zigzag below.

b, A section of the same moulding.

c, A string, consisting of a fillet and the hatched moulding.

d, A representation of part of a circle of beasts' heads, with their beaks over the round.

PLATE X.

Part of a Norman interior, showing one side of the nave, with the triforium and clerestory windows; and a wooden roof open to the rafters. The piers are the massive circular piers, with ornamented arches; the windows are varied, as are the divisions of the triforium, to show the different modes of arrangement in this style: through one of the arches is shown the roof of the side aisle.

The lower portion is a roof and battlements, with a cornice, and the pedestals of pinnacles. On the left hand, the common battlement, with the capping running only horizontally. In the centre, a division with several descriptions of pierced battlement, and the capping running round. On the right hand, the battlement with one moulding running round, and the capping running only horizontally.

PLATE XI.

An Early English composition, with a double door and shafts, with leaved capitals and bands; an ornamented circle above the centre of the doors. The buttresses are nearly those of Salisbury cathedral, as well as the pannelling in, and the arches under, the parapet.

Above, is an ornamented division of three windows, and below, one plain one; at the end is a flying

buttress. On each side over the door, are circular
sunk pannels with ornamented points.

PLATE XII.

The west end of a Decorated building. This has
square corner buttresses, which terminate with octagonal pedestals for pinnacles. These buttresses are of
three stages; the lowest have in front triangular crocketed heads, and square sunk niches. The second stage
is plain, with plain moulded set-offs; the upper stage
is pannelled, and with triangular crocketed heads.
The parapet is plain, and the cornice flowered. The
window is set on a tablet, which runs round the
buttresses, and is of seven lights, with architrave of
mouldings, dripstone, and canopy, supported by
figures. The canopy is triangular, and crocketed; the
interval filled with tracery in sunk pannels. The
door-way consists of mouldings set on the lower base-
tablet, and a plain dripstone, supported by heads.
The door is covered with ornamental iron-work. The
base mouldings consist of two tablets, an ogee, and
plain slope.

PLATE XIII.

A composition showing a Decorated interior, with
three aisles, all of the same height, and groined. The
piers are of the late slender description, and the groins
at the sides rise from single shafts, setting down on a
stone seat, which goes round the aisles. At the end
are three niches, with pedestals and ogee canopies, and
over them a circular window with flowing tracery.
In the wall of the aisle is shown a stoup, and in front
a font raised on steps.

PLATE XIV.

A Perpendicular porch set against the aisles of a building, of which part of two windows are seen. This porch has buttresses of three stages, set square, and leaving a corner, on which is placed a battlemented pinnacle. The buttresses have moulded set-offs. The door-way has an arch within a square, the spandrels pannelled and flowered, and the dripstone running as a tablet, but not round the buttresses. The inner door-way plain-arched, and a plain dripstone. Over the door are two heights of pannelling up to the gable, in seven lights, with a battlemented transom, and a line of square quatrefoils. The parapet pannels consist of round quatrefoils, in squares; the capping crocketed, and running up to flank a cross, of which the pedestal appears springing from the cornice. The cornice is plain. The base mouldings consist of three tablets.

a, Section of the architrave mouldings of a door in the ruins of Birkenhead priory, in Cheshire, a singularly varied and very beautiful specimen of Decorated mouldings.

b, One variety of the Tudor flower.

c, Part of the pier mouldings of St. Michael's, at Coventry;—a specimen of Perpendicular mouldings.

PLATE V.

T.Rickman del.

W.Radclyffe sc.

Published by J & J. Smith, Liverpool, 1 July, 1817.

Printed by W & J Radclyffe.

PLATE VI.

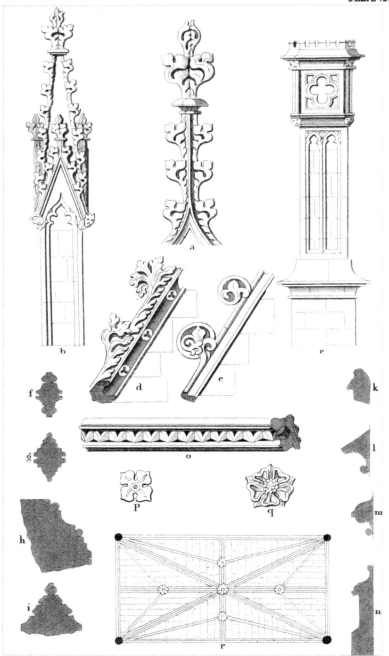

T. Rickman del.

W. Radclyffe sc.

Published by J & J. Smith, Liverpool. 1 July. 1817.

Printed by W & T. Radclyffe.

PLATE VII.

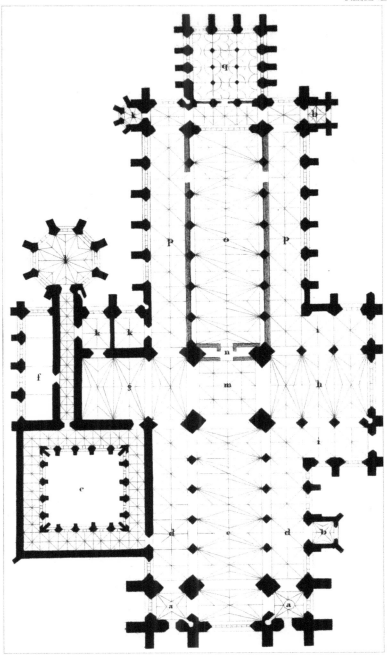

T.Rickman del.

T.Radclyffe sc.

Published by J & J. Smith, Liverpool, 1 July, 1817.

Printed by W & T.Radclyffe.

PLATE VIII.

T.Rickman del.

W.Radclyffe sc.

Published by J & J. Smith, Liverpool. 1 July. 1817.

Printed by W & T. Radclyffe.

PLATE IX.

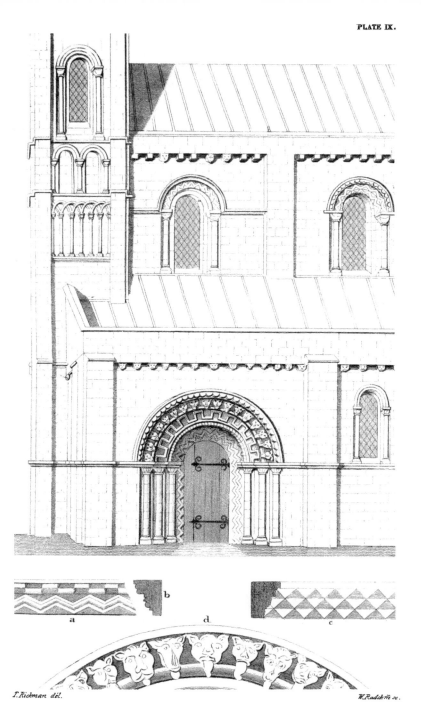

a   b   d   c

T. Rickman del.   W. Radclyffe sc.

Published by J & J. Smith, Liverpool, 1 July, 1817.

Printed by W & T. Radclyffe.

PLATE X.

NORMAN INTERIOR

T. Rickman del.

W. Radclyffe sc.

Published by J & J. Smith. Liverpool. 1 July. 1817.

Printed by W & T. Radclyffe.

PLATE XI.

T.Rickman del.

W.Radclyffe sc.

EARLY ENGLISH.

Published by J & J Smith, Liverpool, 1 July. 1817.

PLATE XII.

T.Rickman del.

W.Radclyffe sc.

Published by J & J. Smith, Liverpool, 1 July, 1817.

Printed by W & T.Radclyffe.

PLATE XIV.

PERPENDICULAR ENGLISH.

a

b

c

T. Rickman del.

W. Radclyffe sc.

Published by J. & J. Smith. Liverpool. 1. July. 1817.

Printed by W. & T. Radclyffe.

ENUMERATION OF BUILDINGS,

PRINCIPLES OF ENGLISH ARCHITECTURE.

Bedfordshire.

DUNSTABLE CHURCH. The remains of the ancient priory is the principal object of curiosity in this county. Its general arrangement is Norman, and it appears to consist of the nave only of the priory church. The windows have been mostly filled with late tracery, and it is the west front which forms the great object of attention; this is a curious piece of patchwork, containing the old Norman central door-way, built up and filled with a Perpendicular door and ornaments. The other part contains various gradations of Early and Decorated English. The Norman work is a good specimen, both as to ornaments and the interior composition.

LUTON CHURCH has a fine tower of alternate checkers of flint and stone, and is curious for its baptistry, or chapel over the font, and a beautiful pierced double arch in the chancel; this is of late Perpendicular, but the principle may be valuable in modern work.

CLAPHAM CHURCH has a tower which appears very ancient, and of which particular mention has been made in a former part of this work.

FELMERSHAM CHURCH has a beautiful west end; it is Early English, and forms a composition very beautiful and not very common.

The other churches which may be mentioned are, those of Elstow, Leighton Buzzard, Toddington, and Wimington.

Berkshire.

ST. GEORGE'S CHAPEL, in the castle of Windsor, one of the finest Perpendicular buildings in the kingdom. This building is perfectly regular in its plan, and, except the remains of a much earlier wall, and one door at the east end, all in one style. It is a most valuable edifice for study, but care must be taken to distinguish between the ancient work and the modern restorations, or rather additions, which include the altar screen, some of the work of the stalls, the organ screen, the font, and several smaller parts. The west end of this chapel is a very fine specimen of a large Perpendicular window.

SHOTTESBROOKE CHURCH is a beautiful miniature cross church, of good design; it is late Decorated work.

AVINGTON CHURCH has a Norman arch of singular shape, dividing the chancel from the nave; it is a portion of two arches, and being more than a quadrant of each circle, it forms an obtuse depending point in the middle.

WELFORD CHURCH is a curious little remain, containing all the styles—a rude Norman round tower supports an Early English stage above it, and a Decorated English spire, and the body of the church contains Perpendicular work.

ABINGDON. A portion of St. Helen's church has five divisions, or what, in foreign churches, is frequently called five naves; that is, an additional side aisle on each side.

Other churches that may be mentioned are, those of St. Nicholas, Abingdon; St. Mary's and St. Lawrence's, Reading; Faringdon, Padworth, Shillingford, Sparsholt, Thatcham, Tidmarsh, and Windsor; and the Abbey-gate at Abingdon, though mutilated, still remains.

Buckinghamshire.

STEWKLEY CHURCH is an object of curiosity, as well for its being a good Norman structure, as for its having been heretofore almost constantly cited as a Saxon church, although there does not appear any real evidence of its erection before the Conquest; and there is nothing about it to distinguish it from many churches known to be erected after the Conquest.

ETON COLLEGE CHAPEL is a specimen of late Perpendicular, but its interior is disfigured by Roman admixtures of screen-work.

MAID'S MORTON CHURCH has some stalls highly enriched.

Other churches——Chetwode, Dinton, Haversham, Hillesdon, Great and Little Marlow, Upton, and Water Stratford.

Cambridgeshire.

ELY CATHEDRAL is of course the first object in this county. It contains nearly a complete series of examples; some valuable Norman work in the older parts, and adjacent buildings of Early English, of several gradations; Decorated work of most excellent execution, and good Perpendicular. The central lantern is the finest in the kingdom of its kind; its composition very bold, and its execution extremely delicate. Trefoil niches, with pedestals of foliage and ogee canopies, form an ornament under the windows, of singular beauty. There are some restorations which require to be distinguished from the original work.

KING'S COLLEGE CHAPEL, Cambridge, the flower of Cambridge, and in many respects of the Perpendicular style, needs little description; simple in its plan, bold in its elevation, rich in its detail, and exquisite in its execution, it must be seen and studied to be properly appreciated.

CAMBRIDGE UNIVERSITY affords not much besides of architectural purity. The ante-chapel of Jesus College has some Early English appearance, but the rest of the colleges present very late work, when the Perpendicular style was struggling with the introduction of the Italian mode.

ST. SEPULCHRE'S CHURCH, Cambridge, is curious as a Norman building, and as one of the few round churches.

ST. MARY'S CHURCH, Cambridge, amidst much addition and alteration, presents, in the divisions of the nave, a good specimen of Perpendicular arrangement.

ST. MICHAEL, ST. BOTOLPH, and ST. PETER'S CHURCHES, in Cambridge, may also be noticed. WHITTLESEA CHURCH has a very fine spire, and THORNEY ABBEY a front with a fine window. The roof of WILLINGHAM CHAPEL has been mentioned before.

Other churches——Babraham, Camps, Swavesey, Sawston, and Trumpington.

Cheshire.

CHESTER CATHEDRAL. This edifice, though its exterior seldom attracts the attention it deserves, from the decay of the stone, and the destruction of battlements and pinnacles, yet, to those who will take the pains to examine its composition, it presents a fine series of very good work. The Norman portions are small, but the chapter-house, its vestibule, and a passage beside it, the lady-chapel, and some portions adjoining the north aisle of the choir, present varied and excellent specimens of Early English. The transition to Decorated work may be traced, and the completion of that style in the south transept, and parts of the nave, with the organ screen, is very well marked. The bishop's throne was once the shrine of Saint Werburgh, and deserves peculiar attention. It is of pure Decorated character, and though disfigured by paint, it is in excellent preservation. The west end, the south porch, the cloisters, the upper part of the nave and transepts, and the central tower, are Perpendicular work, mostly of good character, and the stalls and tabernacle-work are peculiarly fine.

ST. JOHN'S CHURCH, Chester, presents a very fine specimen of Norman and Early English, and the tower has been a very rich Perpendicular one; but the perishable nature of the stone is such, that nearly all traces of the once excellent pannelling are lost.

NANTWICH CHURCH contains some excellent work; the stalls are fine, and there are several good windows; the tower, a small octagon over the intersection of the cross, is simple and elegant; and the east end presents a fine composition of buttresses, canopy, and battlements.

BEBBINGTON CHURCH is a curious mixture of plain Norman, with a fine eastern portion of good Perpendicular work.

BIRKENHEAD PRIORY, in ruins, has in the chapel, in vaults, and in the door-ways, some very good work. The mouldings of the door-ways are of very excellent composition.

RUNCORN CHURCH contains good plain Early English work, and good wood carvings.

The churches of MALPAS, MACCLESFIELD, and WITTON, have all of them parts, the composition of which is curious.

Other churches——Audlem, Great Budworth, Frodsham, Middlewich, and Little Peover.

Cornwall.

LAUNCESTON CHURCH, though not very excellent in its composition, is yet curious for the very great profusion of ornament. The south porch, and some parts adjacent, are literally covered with pannels and carvings.

PROBUS TOWER is a fine specimen of a Perpendicular tower.

ST. GERMAIN'S has a good Norman front, but there appears nothing to warrant a supposition that its age is so great as that assigned to it by the learned and elaborate Whitaker.

Other churches——Truro, Morvinstone, Kilkhampton, and Cury; Egloshayle has a curious stone pulpit.

Cumberland.

CARLISLE CATHEDRAL, though mutilated, is still deserving of much attention ; its eastern end is peculiarly fine. The window is by far the most free and brilliant example of Decorated tracery in the kingdom. The roof is good, and the general Early English arrangement very fine.

LANERCOST ABBEY and CHURCH, though partly in ruins, is yet in sufficient preservation to show its composition to have been excellent, both in its Norman and Early English parts.

PENRITH CHURCH may also be mentioned.

Derbyshire.

ALL SAINT'S CHURCH, Derby, has a tower of uncommon beauty; it is late, but its composition is very good, and it is not very like any other tower in the kingdom.

Other churches——Ashbourn, Bakewell, Bonsal, Chesterfield, Ilam, and Matlock.

Devonshire.

EXETER CATHEDRAL. The nave and choir of this cathedral present one uniform arrangement of simple elegance. The work is plain, but very good ; it is of the Decorated style, and the windows are very various in their tracery, perhaps the most varied of any building in England, and some of them very excellent. The eastern window is a Perpendicular one, as are those of the chapter-house, where Perpendicular work has been curiously added to Early English. The plan of this church is curious; the transepts are two very massive towers of Norman work, with various stages of ornamental arches, and a very large window inserted in the lower part of each tower. The screen which forms the west front is very rich, and full of statuary niches; it is of late date, and forms a great contrast to the upper part of this front, which is very plain. There is or was lately remaining, on the ridge of the roof, an ornament in lead much like the Tudor flower, perhaps the only one remaining in England.

ST. MARY OTTERY CHURCH is large, and has two towers in nearly the same situation as Exeter cathedral.

Other churches——Plympton St. Mary's, Paignton, Bishop's Teignton, East Teignmouth, and Totness.

Dorsetshire.

ST. MARY'S CHURCH, Sherborne, is a large and fine church; a porch at the west end, on the south, contains some good Norman work; the rest of the church is principally of the Perpendicular style, and of good character. The tower is short and massive, but of good composition.

WIMBORNE MINSTER is a large and not very elegant structure; it has a very massive Norman tower at the intersection of the cross, with a row of plain and one of intersecting arches; and there is also a tower of later date, and not so thick, at the west end.

Durham.

DURHAM CATHEDRAL is a large and noble pile, and from its situation, the vicinity of the palace, and some other buildings, and the surrounding scenery, it is almost unequalled. Its interior (the exterior has been chiseled over,) is very massive, and a fine specimen of Norman. The east end is a series of chapels, once called the nine altars, of elegant Early English; but with tracery of later date put into the windows. There are some fine windows of flowing tracery, and the central tower is of the Perpendicular style. The two western towers are Norman, and there is a low chapel of the same style at the west end. There are some very rich Norman doors in several parts, and a very fine throne and altar-screen, of Decorated or early Perpendicular work.

Other churches —— Dalden, Easington, Hartlepool, Houghton-le-Spring, Pittington, and Staindrop.

Essex.

WALTHAM ABBEY CHURCH, from its size and antiquity, claims the first notice in this county; its arrangement is that of very bold Norman; the present church is only the original nave, and at its west door has a portion of good Decorated work.

SOUTH OCKENDON CHURCH has a very fine Norman door.

GREENSTEAD CHURCH is curious from its construction, being built with chesnut-trees set up lengthwise for the sides.

LITTLE MAPLESTEAD is a round church, and is a most elegant little specimen of the Decorated style, of beautiful composition.

SAFFORN WALDEN, and THAXTED CHURCHES, are very fine examples of late Perpendicular work; the latter has a fine spire.

Other churches——Borking, Chingford, Thundersley, and East Ham.

HEDINGHAM CASTLE contains some good Norman remains.

ST. JOHN'S ABBEY GATE, Colchester, is of good composition.

Gloucestershire.

GLOUCESTER CATHEDRAL is a curious and very magnificent edifice. The principal part is Norman, and the crypts are fine and perfect. The windows have been altered nearly all over the building, but the principal alteration is the casing of the Norman work of the choir, and some other parts, with very rich Perpendicular work, which, from the necessity of retaining various Norman forms, is, in many parts, very curious; at this time also, the tower, one of the most beautiful in the kingdom as to composition and ornament, was erected; and also the lady-chapel, a building of uncommon ornament in the interior, though rather plain on the exterior. The west front, and the very magnificent south porch, are additions, in a very fine style. There are many small parts about this cathedral worthy of equal attention. The monument of king Edward the II, some cells in the north transepts, and various other parts might be mentioned; the entrance to the choir is disgraced by a screen, as barbarous as it is well possible to compose. The cloisters are the richest in England, and seem to have been the first roofs of fan tracery, which is executed here with a freedom and brilliancy more analogous to the Decorated than the Perpendicular style.

TEWKESBURY CHURCH is another noble Norman remain, with various insertions and additions. Here were once some fine cloisters, and the remains of some of the pannelling is still visible.

FAIRFORD CHURCH is said to have been built for the purpose of containing some foreign glass, which was presented to it.

Other churches —— Almondsbury, Arlingham, Avening, Bibury, Charfield, Cheltenham, Cherrington, Cirencester, Cleve, Cold Ashton, Cromhall, Down Amney, Harscomb, Northleach, Siddington, and South Cerney.

Hampshire.

WINCHESTER CATHEDRAL presents a variety of excellent work; its general basis was Norman, but like many others, it has been much altered. The transepts and centre tower remain nearly in their original state. The nave appears to have been cased on the original Norman piers, or to accommodate its appearance to the massiveness of that style, to have been worked in a style of peculiar strength. The west end has three fine porches of a singular kind, plain pannelling on the outside, and rich groining on the interior. East of the present choir is a portion which is a very fine specimen of Early English. The choir itself, and an additional east chapel, is good Perpendicular; the piers seem very early. There are several monumental chapels, and monuments of different dates, principally very rich Perpendicular work.

ROMSEY CHURCH, CHRIST-CHURCH, Twiname, and the HOSPITAL of ST. CROSS, near Winchester, are three very fine specimens of Norman work, with various later additions; and St. Cross presents some curious gradations and singularities of Norman.

NETLEY ABBEY, though in ruins, still presents some very fine Early English composition.

SHALFLEET CHURCH, in the Isle of Wight, and some other churches, contain detached parts worth examining.

Herefordshire.

HEREFORD CATHEDRAL. The west end of this cathedral, which had two Norman towers, fell down in 1786, and the reparations consequent on this accident, have much altered the nave, of which the lower part is Norman, with massive round piers; the rest of the building is principally Norman, but much altered by introductions and additions, particularly windows. The extreme east end has been a fine specimen of Early English, but is now much mouldered. There is an additional cloister leading from some of the outbuildings, beside the usual cloisters. The chapter-house is destroyed.

Other churches——Leominster, Madely, and Ross.

Hertfordshire.

ST. ALBAN'S ABBEY CHURCH. This magnificent pile is principally Norman, of a very bold plain character; but it also contains, in its various parts, many gradations of style even to very late work, and some of it very good; but many reparations have been made of very inferior character.

Other churches——Abbot's Langley, King's Langley, Aldenham, Berkhampsted, Broxbourne, and Bushey.

Huntingdonshire.

ST. NEOT'S CHURCH has a fine tower of late Perpendicular, with some singularities, but on the whole a fine composition.

Other churches —— All Saints, Huntingdon ; Buckden, Godmanchester, Kimbolton, and St. Ives.

Kent.

CANTERBURY CATHEDRAL. This most extensive and magnificent edifice contains examples of style, which (including monuments and small parts) form almost a continued series of gradation, from Early Norman to very late Perpendicular; its buildings in immediate connection with the cathedral, are nearly complete, and it has a more than ordinary diversity of chapels. The plan of this cathedral, westward of the centre tower, is not uncommon. Two towers form the flanks of the west end of the nave, to the northern side of which the cloisters are attached. The portion, eastward of the centre tower, is curious from the diversity of its parts; behind the altar in the choir, the two next arches are set sloping, so as to narrow the middle aisle of Trinity-chapel, and place the side chapels on a slope also. The eastern part of Trinity-chapel is circular, and has attached to it, eastward, a circular chapel called Becket's crown. The eastern portion of the buildings is mostly Norman, with Early English upper parts, and mixed variously with the Norman, of which style the eastern transept principally consists. Several of the chapels have the eastern part circular. The western transept, the nave, cloisters, and south-west tower, are all good Perpendicular work. The north-west tower is Norman. The cloisters, though deprived of their pinnacles, battlements, and part of their canopies, are still fine; and the large window at the west end of the chapter-house adds much to their appearance. Of the chapels, that of king Henry the IV. must be noticed as a beautiful piece of Perpendicular work; it is simple, but the roof is an excellent specimen of fan tracery. St. Anselm's chapel has had introduced a very fine Decorated window. There are several other chapels which claim attention, and the church is very rich in monuments. The crypt is extensive, and from its variety, very curious. The general exterior appearance of the church is magnificent, from its very fine central tower; and a judicious addition of pinnacles to the north-west tower, would add much to the general effect. Attached to the south-west tower is a rich and beautiful porch. The entrance gate, called Christ-church gate, is a good specimen of late Perpendicular.

ST. AUGUSTINE'S ABBEY. There still remains some part of this building of good character, particularly the fragment of St. Ethelbert's tower, and the gate-house, a very beautiful piece of work.

ROCHESTER CATHEDRAL. This venerable building, though possessing comparatively little diversity, has yet some parts deserving attention; its general arrangement is Norman and Early English, the nave and west end a fine specimen of the former. The door leading to the present chapter-house is a very rich specimen of niches in architrave mouldings. The additional buildings to this church have been mostly destroyed, and there has been much modern casing.

BARFRESTON CHURCH. This curious little Norman church has, like Stewkley, been generally cited as Saxon, and with much the same reason; it has many singularities, of which perhaps the circular east window is one of the greatest.

Other churches —— Beaksbourne and Westwell; St. Mary's, Dover; St. Clement's, Sandwich; Minster and St. Peter's, in the Isle of Thanet; New Romney; St. Mildred's, Canterbury; and Malling Abbey. The remains of St. Andrew's priory, Rochester, and Eltham palace, may also be mentioned.

Lancashire.

MANCHESTER OLD CHURCH, though the whole is of late Perpendicular, and some very bad reparations were made some years back, yet, from the very careful restoration it appears now to be undergoing, and the valuable screen-work and cieling of the choir, is becoming increasingly deserving of attention. The tower is fine, and the stall-work in the choir excellent; and of its own dark colour without paint. The church is very large, and from the addition of chapels, forms in the western part five aisles, and accommodates a very large congregation.

WARRINGTON CHURCH. The arches of the central tower are good Perpendicular, and the chancel Decorated work of good character; but all the rest of the church, except a portion of the north transept, has been rebuilt in a most barbarous style.

HALSALL CHURCH. The north aisle and north wall of the chancel, and east end window of the south aisle, are all of Decorated character, and in the chancel is a fine canopy over a tomb of this style. The rest of the chancel is early Perpendicular work of excellent execution; and of rather later date, is the tower and spire, and the arches of the nave. There are no clerestory windows, and the roof, which appears original, has three flowered mouldings, one at the point, and the others at the spring of a plain arch. The exterior of this chancel has been executed in a very careful manner.

LANCASTER CHURCH has not much to attract notice, (though part of the interior is good Perpendicular,) except the very fine carved wood-work before noticed. The tower of this church, from its height, looks well at a distance, but is in reality a most barbarous composition.

Other churches —— Cartmel, Winwick, and Holland chapel. There are considerable remains of Furness Abbey, and some of Cockersand.

Leicestershire.

ALL SAINTS, and ST. MARY'S, Leicester; and the churches of Loughborough, Melton Mowbray, and Oadby.

Lincolnshire.

LINCOLN CATHEDRAL. This noble edifice, from its singular situation, is seen over a great extent of country, and its three towers have a very fine effect. The west and east fronts have already been noticed. The division of the Norman work, and later additions to the western towers, are very plain. The nave is very fine, and the piers peculiarly rich. The proportions of the nave and side aisles are such as do not often occur, the aisles being remarkably narrow, but the whole has an exellent effect. The view of the transept is very fine, and the lantern is good, though rather obscure, from the small size of the windows. At each end of the transept is a circular window, the north a good Early English one, the south one of the finest

K

Decorated circles remaining. This window is set in an arch of open stone-work, which is nearly, if not quite, unequalled. The screen under the organ is one of the finest examples of late Early English work; it has some little resemblance to the character of queen Eleanor's crosses, but its principal beauty is in the workmanship of the bands of open foliage, round the doors. The walling of the arches is filled with square flowers, and these have been painted and gilt, traces of which still remain. The arrangement of the intersection of the smaller eastern transept is very good, and adds much to the beauty of the choir. Some beautiful small chapels are attached to the lady-chapel, and the south door is peculiarly elegant. Three sides of the cloisters, of good Decorated work, remain in their original state; the fourth is a modern library. From the eastern side of the cloisters is the passage to the chapter-house, which is a decagon, and though not equal to Salisbury, it is yet very fine. Marks of the Roman operations are remarkably clear at Lincoln. The north gate of this city is the Roman arch still retaining its original use; in the wall of the castle is another arch walled up, but evidently Roman; and in the midst of the area of the cloisters, some feet below the surface, is a fine Tessellated pavement. To all this it may be added, that the north road, towards Brigg and Barton, continues in a straight line for many miles.

BOSTON CHURCH claims the next attention, as the highest, and one of the finest Perpendicular towers in the kingdom. The church itself contains good Decorated work. The tower is simple in its composition, but rich, from being completely pannelled; and on its top rises a fine lantern of open-work.

THORNTON ABBEY, and CROYLAND ABBEY, both contain remains of very good work; and near the latter is the celebrated triangular bridge, which seems evidently of Decorated workmanship.

LOUTH CHURCH presents a very fine specimen of good Perpendicular work. The tower and spire are very elegant, both in proportion and execution, and the east window is a composition of more boldness and simplicity than is usually met with.

GRANTHAM CHURCH has a very fine spire.

SLEAFORD CHURCH contains portions of all the styles, the Decorated part particularly fine, especially the windows, and a door.

BRENT BROUGHTON, near Newark, is a beautiful little church.

BARTON. Two churches have been noticed in another part, when speaking of the probability of Saxon remains. The tower of the new church is a piece of good Early English.

FOLKINGHAM CHURCH has a tower of late Perpendicular work, of which the battlements, pinnacles, and a band under them, are very elegant.

STAMFORD contains several churches of different styles, worthy of great attention, particularly the Early English parts. St. Martin's, Stamford Baron, is of good Perpendicular work, and contains several tombs of the Cecils, in the mixed Italian style. The small remains of the White-friar's gate, and St. Leonard's hospital, are curious pieces of composition.

Other churches——Clee, Colby, Freston, Kirton, Ketton, Great Grimsby, Market Raisin; Stoke Rochford; Silk Willoughby, and Stow.

London.

Although various causes have contributed to strip the Metropolis of ancient English edifices, and particularly that wide desolater, the fire of 1666, there are yet remaining some very curious specimens.

The CHAPEL in the White Tower, now the Record Room, is one of the most complete specimens of a Norman church, on a small scale, which remains; and in some other parts of the White Tower are Early English remains.

The CHURCH of ST. BARTHOLOMEW the GREAT, in West Smithfield, contains much good Norman work, and its entrance gate, from Smithfield, is Early English, with the toothed ornament in its mouldings.

The TEMPLE CHURCH, of which the mixed part has been mentioned before, and is one of the best of the few round churches. The eastern part is a most excellent specimen of plain light Early English, and its groining and slender piers are perhaps unequalled.

The DUTCH CHURCH, Austin Friars, contains some very good Decorated windows.

The end of ELY CHAPEL, fronting Ely-place, has one fine Decorated window of curious composition.

The CHURCH of ST. CATHARINE, near the Tower, though sadly disfigured by alterations of various dates, still contains several parts worthy of attention, particularly in the eastern portion.

ST. JOHN'S GATE, Clerkenwell, is Perpendicular work of pretty good character.

The front of GUILDHALL CHAPEL, though much decayed and disfigured, is a good piece of pannelling. Guildhall itself has been so altered that it can hardly be now considered an ancient building.

The remains of CROSBY HALL, Bishopsgate-street, are so very excellent in their kind, that it is a pity they cannot be restored to their original state: erected as a domestic mansion, they furnish many good hints for modern work, and the details are as good as any Perpendicular work remaining of the kind.

Middlesex.

WESTMINSTER ABBEY. This building has been too often figured and described to need much notice in this place. The general arrangement is of an elegant and valuable description of Early English, and it would have been well if Sir C. Wren had extracted from the building before him, (which he might have done, even if he had not consulted other buildings, which we know, from his remarks on Salisbury, he had an opportunity to do,) principles to have adapted his towers to their lower part, instead of introducing a barbarous mixture, which has no likeness to any thing except his own barbarisms at Oxford. As Britons, we cannot regret the use of this most magnificent pile, though as architects we may regret that the principles of English architecture have not been more attended to in those (taken as insulated pieces,) admirable efforts of the sculptor's art, which are spread over these walls. The Corinthian altar-piece of marble, in the choir, would be a valuable present to some Grecian church, and if replaced by an appropriate composition, would harmonize a choir now rendered very discordant.

The cloisters of the abbey are fine specimens of tracery, and some of the additional buildings deserve more attention than is usually paid them.

Of HENRY the VII.'s CHAPEL it is difficult to speak in proper terms ;— as a magazine of parts, one of the most valuable in the kingdom ; as a whole, a mass of frittered ornament. The porch, which is seldom to be seen for want of light, is one of the most chaste and beautiful vestibules of the style, and many of the parts of the chapel, taken separately, are unequalled. The tomb of Henry the VII. sufficiently shows how early a degree of debasement took place.

The exterior of this building has been under repair, and parts are added which have not existed for many years past.

WESTMINSTER HALL. The roof, and west end of this building, are very fine. The niche-work on each side of the door, covered up for many years, is as good a specimen of Perpendicular niche-work as any extant. The walls of this building to the bottom of the windows, appear to be Norman. There were many curious remains in the adjacent buildings, but the late additions and alterations have taken away or hidden the greatest part of them.

The Parish churches within a circuit of from twenty to thirty miles round the metropolis, are, with a very few exceptions, small and poor buildings; and the following list in this county will be found to contain only a small portion of good work in most of them: Bedfont, Greenford, Hadley, Hanworth, Harlington, Hillingdon, Harrow-on-the-Hill, Ickenham, Rislip, South Mims, and Stanwell.

Monmouthshire.

ST. THOMAS S CHURCH, Monmouth. LLANTHONY ABBEY

Norfolk.

NORWICH CATHEDRAL. This venerable pile presents a variety of styles, and some of its parts are of great value. The nave, central tower, and eastern portion, present a continued line of Norman work of excellent character, and with not much alteration except in the windows and the roof; the latter is of Perpendicular character, as is the centre of the west front, the door, and large west window. The east end is circular, and is a very fine composition ; in its aisles are some good Norman groined roofs. Parts of the choir arches have been filled up and altered with rich Perpendicular work of good character. The tower, both inside and out, presents one of the best specimens of Norman ornament extant. The spire is good, of Decorated or early Perpendicular character. The cloisters are large and fine, and comprise a curious series of work, from early Decorated to middle Perpendicular; and the gradation is easily observed in the character of the tracery, though something of the same general forms are preserved; there is a very fine door, and some lavatories of very good work, in these cloisters. There are some remains of good work about the ancient buildings of the bishop's palace, and a very rich late Perpendicular gate at the western entrance to the cathedral.

Some of the other churches in Norwich, particularly St. Peter's, Mancroft, deserve attention.

LYNN contains four buildings, all valuable, St. Mary's church, St. Nicholas's chapel, the Greyfriars, and the Red-mount chapel. This last is so beautiful a specimen of small interior work, that it is much to be wished that some care may be taken, at least to preserve, if not to restore it.

At Walsingham, the ruins of the PRIORY, and the beautiful font in the church, have already been mentioned.

BINHAM PRIORY; the west end is a good specimen of Early English, the interior is Norman.

ATTLEBURGH has some good windows.

CASTLE ACRE PRIORY has a west front of very rich Norman work, and some of the adjacent buildings are curious.

Other churches——Houghton-le-Dale, Swaffham, Shottisham, and Walpole.

Northamptonshire.

PETERBOROUGH CATHEDRAL. The approach to this cathedral has a very monastic appearance. Passing under a Norman gate, with later additions, a court is entered, the right side of which is a line of the domestic buildings of the abbey, still retaining much of their original appearance; at the end of the court is the noble front of the cathedral, consisting of three fine Early English arches, but their beauty is much diminished by the small chapel or porch, which, in another place, would have been very beautiful. The general arrangement of this building is Norman, but nearly all the windows have had tracery inserted, and in some parts, the windows enlarged. The east end is circular, and the aisles are made out square by a Perpendicular addition, which has some excellent fan tracery groining. This work is plain in its exterior appearance, and the buttresses have sitting statues instead of pinnacles. The choir has a wooden groined roof, of very inferior workmanship and appearance. The central tower is low, and forms a lantern. The screen is a barbarous piece of painted wood-work. A very small part of the back arches (apparently a lavatory) of the cloisters remains, and there is a portion of arch-work near, of very good Early English character, most likely the hall or refectory of the convent. The north-eastern pier of the central tower is decayed, and kept together with several bands of iron.

QUEEN'S CROSSES, at Geddington and Northampton, have been before mentioned.

NORTHAMPTON, St. Peter's, is a curious Norman remain, much of it in its original state.

ST. SEPULCHRE'S is one of the round churches, and appears the latest, except Little Maplestead; it has a tower of later work added to it, and a pretty good spire.

ST. GILES'S contains some good work of several styles.

HIGHAM FERRARS. The spire and upper part of the tower have been rebuilt, but the west door and shallow porch are curious specimens of good Decorated work; the composition of the door is not common, being double, with flat arches. There is a Perpendicular school-house near the church, and a ruined chapel of the bead-house.

IRTLINGBOROUGH CHURCH has an Early English tower, and on it an octagonal lantern of later date.

Other churches —— Barnack, King's Sutton, Oundle, Raunds, Stanwick, Thrapstone, Twywell, and Woodford.

Northumberland.

ST. NICHOLAS, Newcastle. This church contains several good parts, but its chief excellence is its beautiful tower and lantern spire; a building imitated in various parts, but equalled by none. The spire is supported on arches, which spring from the octagonal turrets at the corners. The work is Perpendicular, plain, but of very good character.

TYNEMOUTH PRIORY. The east end shows, though in ruins, an admirable piece of Early English composition.

LANDISFARNE is in ruins, but still retains some curious and excellent Norman work.

HEXHAM CHURCH, though only part remains, shows some good work in several styles.

Nottinghamshire.

The COLLEGIATE CHURCH of Southwell is a cross church of considerable magnitude. The nave and cross, the two towers at the west end, and the central tower, are all Norman; that of the nave is very massive. The choir is Early English, of good character; and it has a screen of good Decorated work; on the north side is the chapter-house, an octagon of very good Decorated character, the entrance to which is by a double door, with some very rich flowered mouldings in the architrave. At the west end of the nave, a large Perpendicular window has been introduced.

The remains of NEWSTEAD ABBEY are sufficiently perfect to deserve attention.

The CHURCH and GATE, Worksop, have parts of good character in their respective styles.

The CHURCH at Newark is one of the largest and finest parish churches in the kingdom. The plan is of considerable breadth. The tower and spire rise engaged in the west end, the lower part Early English, the upper part has been before described. The south aisle is Decorated, of excellent workmanship, and the window at the west end of this aisle is one of the most beautiful six-light Decorated windows in the kingdom. The eastern part is Perpendicular, of very good workmanship; the buttresses are very light and elegant. The windows various and good, the heads of many of the smaller divisions feathered, straight without an arch, in the manner so common in this part of the kingdom. There is a fine font, and much good work in the interior; the roof of the aisles is flat, and looks very well. On the whole this church deserves a much more minute examination and description than it has yet obtained.

Other churches——Balderton, Retford, and St. Mary's, Nottingham.

Oxfordshire.

The CATHEDRAL of CHRIST-CHURCH, which is the chapel of the college, and the cathedral of the diocese, claims the first notice. It is a Norman building, of singular character, from the disposition of its arches, which are double, a lower one springing from corbels attached to the piers; part of the nave has been demolished, and many windows of late date inserted in different parts. The roof of the choir is a curious and beautiful groined roof, with pendants; on the north side of the choir are some chapels of later character than the rest of the church, and the northernmost one, called the Latin chapel, has some Decorated windows. Part of the cloisters remain; they are of Perpendicular character, and the chapter-house is a very beautiful and valuable specimen of Early English. The tower is in the centre of the cross, and is a plain Early English one with a spire.

ST. MARY'S CHURCH. This is a large Perpendicular building, with a good spire placed in a situation not common, viz on the north side of the nave. The nave is fitted up for the university, with ascending seats, and the chancel part shut off by a screen; on the south side is one of the early attempts at Corinthian, a porch with twisted columns.

ST. PETER'S in the east. This church has a Norman crypt, and some part of the walls are of the same age, but there has been many additions and introductions; the south door is a good one, and some parts of the interior have Norman groins, with the ribs much ornamented. This is one of the churches which have been called Saxon.

The CHURCH of ST. MARY MAGDALEN, at the end of Broad-street, is a small church little noticed, but has some good windows, very elegant buttresses and niches, and the Decorated pierced parapet with a waving line.

Many of the COLLEGES exhibit in their gateways, halls, and chapels, specimens of late Perpendicular work; and several, that intermixture of Italian which took place in the reign of James the I.

The DIVINITY SCHOOL has a very fine roof with pendants.

MERTON COLLEGE CHAPEL exhibits some good Decorated and Perpendicular windows, and the tower is a fine specimen of Perpendicular work.

MAGDALEN COLLEGE CHAPEL has been new roofed by James Wyatt. The tower has before been mentioned. There is a late Perpendicular door, curious from an ornamental arch of stone, standing free in a square head.

NEW COLLEGE CHAPEL has had much modern alteration, but enough remains of the ancient work to show the excellence of its composition.

CHRIST-CHURCH has had much modern alteration, and the principal front is a barbarous mixture, by Sir Christopher Wren.

ALL SOULS has another portion as barbarous, by Nicholas Hawksmoor.

IFFLEY CHURCH is a very valuable specimen of Norman; it has three rich doors, and a good short tower, with battlements of much later date. The eastern portion is Early English, and some Decorated and Perpendicular windows have been introduced. This church has been called Saxon.

DORCHESTER CHURCH has some curious Decorated windows, particularly one with a genealogical tree worked in the mullions and appendages.

Other churches——Burford, Ensham, Henley, Witney, Adderbury, Bloxham, and Ewelm.

Rutlandshire.

TICKENCOTE CHURCH, near Stamford. This church has been partially rebuilt, but the interior of the chancel is original, and the division-arch is a very deep one, with varied and singular mouldings. The outside of the chancel has been rebuilt so as to be nearly, but not exactly, like the old church, and therefore requires great discrimination.

Other churches——Essendine, Market Overton, Okeham, and Uppingham.

Shropshire.

SHREWSBURY ABBEY CHURCH. The basis of this church is Norman, but it is much reduced in size, and many alterations have been made, particularly the introduction of a very large Perpendicular window over the west door.

BUILDWAS ABBEY, WENLOCK ABBEY, and LUDLOW CASTLE, present some very good remains, principally Norman and Early English.

SHIFNALL CHURCH is principally Norman, with some good later windows.

Other churches——St. Mary's, Shrewsbury; Hodnet, Morton Corbet, and Shawbirch.

Somersetshire.

The ABBEY CHURCH at Bath. This building has been before referred to; there is a small portion of Norman wall, with the exception of which the church is a uniform Perpendicular building of very late date, very plain, yet in many respects elegant, but much dilapidated of pinnacles, &c. The curious representation of Jacob's dream, on the west front, has been noticed. The central tower is not square, its north and south dimensions being much larger than the east and west. The monumental chapel of Prior Bird, is a beautiful specimen of enriched work, with fine square pannels, and a very good fan tracery roof.

The CATHEDRAL of Bristol. This is principally early Perpendicular work, with windows much resembling Decorated windows. The portions of the cloisters remaining are of varied design, and of late Perpendicular character. There is only the transept and parts eastward, now roofed; and in size and appearance this church yields much to its elegant neighbour St. Mary Redcliffe.

The CATHEDRAL of Wells. This is principally Early English, with a west end, curious for the number of statues remaining. The east window is Perpendicular, and the roof of the choir very rich. The nave is plain, but of good character, and under the western arch of the great tower is a fine reversed arch, forming a very fine screen.

The CHURCH of ST. CUTHBERT, in Wells, is a beautiful Perpendicular building, and its tower curious for the length and construction of the upper windows, which give to the upper half of the tower the lightness of an elegant lantern.

The CHURCH of ST. MARY REDCLIFFE, Bristol, is in many respects superior to the cathedral of Bristol; it is a cross church of considerable size, and of various ages. The tower is Early English, but of late date; some portions of the interior, and the very curious north porch, are Decorated work, but the general appearance of the south side is rich Perpendicular. The groining is very fine, and much of the interior of very excellent execution. The lower part only of the spire remains; about a square of the tower in height, and an ornamented parapet has been added to its top, and some iron-work supporting a vane; it has an awkward appearance, which takes much from the beauty of the church.

TAUNTON CHURCH has a very fine tower, indeed one of the finest in England; it is of late Perpendicular, and very rich.

GLASTONBURY ABBEY and CHURCH contains some beautiful parts. The kitchen of the abbey remains, and is a very curious relic.

ILMINSTER CHURCH has a fine tower, of a light and uncommon construction.

Other churches——Lullington, Bath Easton, and the Temple-church, Bristol.

Staffordshire.

LITCHFIELD CATHEDRAL. The general character of the nave and transept of this church is Early English, but of a curious character; it has not the simplicity of Salisbury cathedral and Westminster abbey, nor the very rich detail of some parts of Lincoln minster, but it approaches in composition, in some parts, much nearer to Decorated work than either of them. In the transepts are various traces of Norman, and the whole has a very rich appearance. The choir is Decorated, of very good character, with later reparations and additions. There is some good Perpendicular niche-work remaining, which has been copied with partial additions for the stalls. The screen is modern, and several modern alterations have taken place. Of the usual additional buildings, this church has only the chapter-house, a beautiful decagon. The east end is hexagonal, and the church has an advantage few possess of being completely insular, and some fine trees not far off, add much to the beauty of its appearance at some distance, and with its three spires, form various beautiful combinations in several directions. The plan of this cathedral is curious; the walls of the nave and choir not being in a straight line, those of the choir inclining a little to the north.

STAFFORD CHURCH is a large cross church of various dates, some good Early English, some Decorated, and some Perpendicular work.

PENKRIDGE has a fine Decorated east window, and some good work in the interior.

WOLVERHAMPTON is a large church, much patched and modernized, but its tower is still a fine one.

Other churches —— Barton-under-Needwood, Abbot's Bromley, Greenhill and Stow, (near Litchfield,) Tutbury, and Uttoxeter.

Suffolk.

The ABBEY-GATE, at Bury St. Edmonds, is, though in a decayed state, a fine specimen of Decorated work. The buttresses are singular, and would lead one to suppose that it was a casing or at least a rebuilding of Norman work

The CHURCH GATE is as good a specimen of Norman, as the other gate is of Decorated work.

ORFORD CHURCH has the remains of some Norman piers, of curious character.

Other churches——Wisset, Brayesworth, and Blithburgh.

Surrey.

LAMBETH PALACE, though hitherto but little noticed as to its architecture, contains many parts worthy of attention; and various gradations from Early English to late Perpendicular. The post-room is curious, as furnishing one of the very few specimens of an ornamented flat cieling.

ST. MARY OVERY, near London-bridge, is a very large church, and deserving of much attention; though its exterior, from various patching, is not very promising, the interior is fine. The nave and lower part of the tower is Early English of late character, and there are various additions to several parts of the later styles, and also introductions of windows. Near this church stood the palace of the bishops of Winchester, which contained a very beautiful circular window of Decorated character; it was superior to most windows of its age, and has been engraved.

Other churches——Beddington and Merton.

Sussex.

CHICHESTER CATHEDRAL. A portion of the walls of the nave of this church is Norman, the rest of the church Early English, but in the nave are two additional aisles of later character, thus making what foreigners call five naves. The tower and spire are fine specimens of plain Early English. The lady-chapel is of later date, as is the north wall of the nave, which has some curious buttresses. The end of the south transept has a fine Decorated window of seven lights, and a beautiful circle over it; there is also a good circle at the east end. There is no detached chapter-house, and the cloisters occupy three sides of an irregular piece of ground, and are placed much eastward of the usual position. The upper part of the north-western tower is destroyed; the south-western tower is plain, its two upper stages plain Early English. Near the west end is a very fine bell tower, which is a very good composition, with a lantern connected by small flying buttresses, with octagonal turrets that spring from the corners above the battlement.

The MARKET CROSS, at Chichester, is an octagon of very beautiful Perpendicular work, with details of great elegance.

WINCHELSEA CHURCH is a Decorated building with a fine monument.

NEW and OLD SHOREHAM CHURCHES contain good Norman work, and the latter some fine Early English.

ARUNDEL CHURCH has some good Decorated work.

Other churches——Boxgrave, Alfriston and Trotton.

Warwickshire.

WARWICK CASTLE, although the apartments in use are modernized, yet, in its outward arrangements and general forms, retains much of the bold outline and grandeur of the ancient abodes of the English nobility. One tower, called Guy's tower, is nearly untouched; it appears to be of Decorated character; though very plain, it is perhaps the most perfect remain of its kind in existence—is very curious both as to composition and construction, and its outline seen from a distance is peculiarly fine.

WARWICK CHURCH. The whole of this church, except the chancel and its adjuncts, is a composition of the greatest barbarity, but the chancel is an uncommonly beautiful specimen of Perpendicular work, and the east front is remarkably fine, simple in its arrangement, yet rich from the elegance of its parts, and the excellent execution of its details. The interior is equally beautiful, and there are, on the north side, a monumental chapel and vestry of very good character; but the great feature of the church is the Beauchamp chapel, an erection whose date, cost, and operative builders, are all well known; it is completely enriched both within and without, its details of the most elegant character and excellent execution, and in very good preservation. It consists of a chapel of several arches, and a small aisle or rather passage on the north side, between the chapel and the chancel of the church. This aisle is arch-roofed in three divisions, each a different pattern; the chapel itself is groined with a flat four-centred arch, and is a very beautiful specimen of composition. At the back of the altar is a small room formed in the projection of the buttresses, which is very great. In the centre of the chapel stands a very rich altar tomb, with the effigies of Richard Beauchamp, earl of Warwick, whose executors erected the chapel; there are some other monuments, but some of the largest of them are of much later date, and rather disfigure the chapel than add to its beauty. The pannelling and minute details of this chapel are remarkably good, and with the adjoining chancel, form an assemblage of various details not often met with.

The city of COVENTRY is very rich in curious building. Of Perpendicular wood-work, there is a great abundance in various parts of the town, particularly one almshouse forming a small square, and a house near St. Mary's hall. The ancient public buildings are also numerous.

ST. MARY'S HALL is the meeting place of the corporation, and is a very curious building; the kitchen, and some other parts, appear much older than the hall itself, which is very excellent Perpendicular work, and it has a small but very beautiful oriel, in which stands a plain but real ancient table. The hall has a fine timber roof, and at the bottom stands a very fine carved oak chair, most parts of which are in excellent preservation. It is much to be regretted that this beautiful and valuable edifice is greatly out of repair; in 1815, a few hundred pounds, judiciously laid out, would have secured it for many years, but if the dilapidations are suffered to continue a few years longer, as many thousands will scarcely suffice.

The present HOUSE of INDUSTRY is a large and irregular collection of buildings, amongst which are all the remains of the WHITE - FRIAR'S MONASTERY, consisting principally of a portion of the cloisters, and some adjacent buildings; these are carefully preserved, (the line of cloister being the dining-room,) and contain some very good specimens of early Perpendicular work. The groining of the cloisters is uncommon, and very beautiful; it is also well adapted for modern plaster-work. There are other detached parts of value, particularly the remains of a gate, and a doorway now blocked up, and a small window placed in it.

The ecclesiastical buildings in COVENTRY are four, exclusive of the remains of the cathedral, which are hardly discernible, and all traces of their details are gone; but they appear to have been Early English.

The GREY FRIAR'S STEEPLE. This beautiful remain stands in a garden, and consists of the central part of a cross church, on which rises a short tower, which becomes octagonal, and has an elegant spire. The small remains of the buildings attached, show it to have been late Early English, but the tower itself is good early Decorated work, with bold mouldings of excellent character; the spire appears to be later.

ST. MICHAEL'S CHURCH. If the stone of which this church was built had been more durable, this would have been the finest Perpendicular steeple in England. The church has many traces of being erected on foundations of earlier date, but it is now all Perpendicular as to general appearance. The steeple is early in the style. The tower has four stages, all of them adorned with niches and pannelling of very excellent character. The spire has several stages, some of which are pannelled; and round the bottom is arranged a lantern, which gives to this spire a peculiar appearance of lightness. The steeple is very high, and when viewed at such a distance as not to show the decayed appearance of the details, is one of the most satisfactory as to its proportions of any in the kingdom. The church is large and undivided; its interior arrangement is fine, from the great breadth of the aisles, and the lightness of the piers. The divisions are pannelled down to the arches, of which pannelling the clerestory windows form part. There is in this church and its vestry, a large collection of stall seats.

TRINITY CHURCH has also a fine spire, and the distance between the two spires not being more than a hundred yards, their combinations at a distance are very fine. This is a cross church, and in many of its parts much resembles St. Michael's, but the design is not so good. In this church is a large stone pulpit.

ST. JOHN'S, or BABLAKE CHURCH, also resembles St. Michael's in the pannelling over the arches, but the clerestory windows are longer and square-headed. There are several singularities about the composition of this church that deserve attention.

STRATFORD-ON-AVON CHURCH has much resemblance in some of its arrangements to the above three churches, but there are parts of much earlier date.

ASTON CHURCH, near Birmingham, has a good tower and spire, but the latter has had some modern alterations; the tower has some of its details so much like those of the chancel at Warwick as to warrant a belief that it may be the work of the same architect.

TAMWORTH CHURCH is large, and contains much curious and excellent work. There is a small portion of Early English, and more Decorated work, but the greatest part is Perpendicular. The tower has a singular double staircase, one from the outside leading to the leads and some other parts, and one from the inside leading to the various stages, but having no communication with the former except at the top.

COLESHILL has a fine spire of late Perpendicular work, of better design than execution. The spire is crocketed, and standing high, is very extensively seen to great advantage.

KENILWORTH CHURCH has some Norman remains.

KENILWORTH CASTLE has extensive remains, some of which are Norman, but the details of most parts remaining are of the age of Elizabeth, or very little earlier.

Westmorland.

In this county may be noticed the churches of KENDAL, BROUGH, and KIRKBY LONSDALE.

Wiltshire.

SALISBURY CATHEDRAL. This edifice is deserving of great attention. It is the only cathedral in England of one style, and completed entirely on one plan, and that plan complete as to all its parts. It is also remarkably free from introductions of later date, for till some late reparations, the organ-screen was of the same date as the church. The only ancient introduction is an arch on each side the nave, to connect the east and west piers of the great tower together. This is Perpendicular work, as is also part of the wooden screen-work; all the rest, except the monuments and modern repairs, is Early English of very excellent character and execution. The north side of this cathedral is well laid open, and the numerous fine trees in the precincts add very much to the effect of its combinations.

The CHURCH of BISHOP CANNING'S has some parts of very good Early English work.

MALMSBURY ABBEY and CROSS, particularly the former, deserve attention; at the abbey are some very fine Norman remains.

Other churches——St. John, and St. James Devizes, Chippenham, Cricklade, and Wotten Basset.

Worcestershire.

WORCESTER CATHEDRAL. The general appearance and arrangements of this church are Early English, with various introductions, particularly windows, most of which are altered. The tower, though, like Salisbury, accommodated to the long lines of the Early English style, has much of Decorated character. The east and west windows are fine, and very large. In the choir is a stone pulpit of remarkably beautiful design. The cloisters are good, and the chapter-house a decagon, Norman, with later windows, and a centre pier. There is a fine Perpendicular porch on the north side.

EVESHAM ABBEY TOWER is a fine Perpendicular remain.

GREAT MALVERN CHURCH has Norman piers, but the exterior is principally Perpendicular, and the tower is remarkably beautiful. The abbey-gate, of Perpendicular date, remains.

PERSHORE CHURCH has some curious Norman parts, and we may also notice those of Little Malvern and Kidderminster.

Yorkshire.

YORK MINSTER. This magnificent cathedral has a portion of all the styles, but the Norman only appears in a fine crypt under part of the choir, which reduces the general appearance to the three latter styles; of these the transepts are Early English; the nave, and arches supporting the great tower, are Decorated, and the choir and upper part of the great tower, are Perpendicular. The cloisters are destroyed, but the chapter-house remains; and at some distance is a building lately restored as a library. The church is much shut up with buildings on the south side; the north is more open, but is not a public passage. There have been so many references to this building in the former part of this work, that less detail will be required here; but it will be proper to remark the excellent effect produced by the great simplicity of composition in the nave. The organ-screen is very fine, and the choir is just so much richer than the nave, as to indicate its superior appropriation. The altar-screen is light and beautiful, and the tabernacle-work of the stalls very good. The lady-chapel is a continuation of the choir on a different level, the altar being much raised. The chapter-house is of Decorated character. and of admirable execution; it is an octagon beautifully groined. The exterior appearance of this church is very fine from its great size, and the excellent effect of its three towers; and in the value of its details, both within and without, it is equalled by few buildings, and exceeded by none.

BEVERLEY MINSTER. This church also has been much referred to; in addition it may be remarked, that its appearance is not benefited by a sort of cupola which forms a very awkward finish for its central tower. The general character of this church is Early English, with many introductions; many windows in the nave are Decorated, and there are several Perpendicular windows, besides those of the east and west fronts. The transepts are very little altered. The choir has a screen which is a strange attempt at mixing Grecian and English work. In the choir is a most beautiful monument of Decorated character, and of most exquisite execution; it is a double arch groined within, and triangular canopies with rich buttressses. The arch is an ogee, double feathered, with tracery between the ogee head and triangle; all the points have heads or half figures, and in the tracery are angels with censers. The spandrels of the featherings are filled with armed figures, bearing shields. Both canopies are richly crocketed; the finial of the upper is tall and very rich; the lower finial is a corbel, on which is a figure, seated in the attitude of benediction; and behind the crockets, about the middle of the upper canopy, are two figures supporting corbels on which are angels. All the small mouldings are filled with the ball ornament, and the whole is in very good preservation, except the tomb, which is plain, and has had some fine brass-work, which is gone. In the north transept is a fine altar-tomb of good Decorated workmanship, and there are several other tombs. In the nave there are Doric galleries in each arch, which, though in themselves not bad, are certainly out of place.

RIPPON MINSTER is a large and venerable edifice, containing various parts worthy of attention, particularly its west front, which is a very fine specimen of bold Early English, and, except the battlements and pinnacles, without alteration.

ST. MARY'S CHURCH, Beverley, if it had not so rich a neighbour as the minster, would be thought a curious and valuable church; its west front is very fine, with beautiful pierced towers, very fine windows, and a door of great beauty, very rich in mouldings, and the hanging feathering. The chancel has some good Decorated work, and some curious groining. The western part is early Perpendicular, and the interior piers and arches very fine.

COTTINGHAM CHURCH, between Hull and Beverley, is a curious small church, with some good Decorated work, and a very excellent Perpendicular chancel; the tower is a light and beautiful design.

144

TRINITY, or the HIGH-CHURCH, at Hull, is a large and fine building; its east end to the street is Decorated, and of good composition; it is a cross church, and in the centre has a very lofty and beautiful tower. The western part is Perpendicular, of good character, remarkably light, and with very small piers. The transepts are of very early Decorated work, and the great window of the south transept is very curious from its tracery and mouldings. Only part of the nave is pewed; the chancel is open, and has a very fine effect; there is in it a Decorated monument, with rich canopy and buttresses.

The LOW CHURCH has some good Perpendicular windows, much like some of the High-church windows.

PAUL, a village on the Humber, below Hull, has a small cross church of good Perpendicular character, and in the south transept is a water-drain in good preservation, with the spout on the outside complete.

HEADON, near Hull, has a very fine church, some parts of which are sadly mutilated, particularly a once fine window in the south transept. A large portion of the church is Early English, of which the front of the north transept is an uncommonly fine specimen. The tower, which is in the centre, is lofty, of good Perpendicular work.

BILTON, a small church or chapel between Headon and Hull, is a curious portion of plain Early English work; the windows are very long and narrow.

SKIRLAW CHAPEL, in Holderness, deserves mention; it was built by Walter Skirlaw, bishop of Durham, and archbishop of York; and is a very beautiful specimen of a Perpendicular chapel; there are parts of it of curious design.

DONCASTER CHURCH is principally remarkable for its tower, the details of which are some of the richest exterior work in the kingdom, particularly the canopies of the buttress stages. The church is a large cross church, mostly of Perpendicular character, but with various traces of earlier work; the interior does not answer the expectations so highly excited by the richness of the exterior.

HOWDEN CHURCH. The east end of this church has already been mentioned, and there are many other parts deserving attention.

The ABBEYS of Whitby, Fountains, Rivaux, Byland, Eastby, Kirkham, Kirkstall, and Richmond, though all in ruins, contain remains which will well repay an examination of them.

On the BRIDGE at Wakefield is a small chapel, the front of which is an elegant specimen of rich Perpendicular work, with canopies and very rich tracery.

CROFTON, near Wakefield, is a small but very neat cross church, of good character.

ADEL, near Leeds, is a good specimen of a Norman church.

Other churches —— Bardsey, Bradford, Godmanham, Guiseley, Haysgarth Halifax, Hemingborough, Malton, Newbald, Pontefract, Richmond, Sherbourne, Selby, Thornhill, and Wakefield, as well as several in the city of York.

In York should also be noticed, the GUILDHALL, and ST. MARY'S ABBEY, which, though in ruins, presents some curious and beautiful details, in an elegant transition from Early English to Decorated work.

Wales.

The Welsh cathedrals of ST. DAVID, LLANDAFF, BANGOR, and ST. ASAPH, though inferior in size and magnificence to most of the English cathedrals, yet all contain parts deserving attention, though amidst much alteration and decay.

The ABBEYS of LLANTHONY, TINTERN, MARGAM, VALLE CRUCIS, and BASINGWERK, though all in ruins, yet contain parts that are valuable both as to composition and detail.

The CHAPEL erected over the celebrated spring at Holywell, is a Perpendicular erection of very great beauty; and as a piece of composition, has rarely been exceeded in the elegance of its groins and niche-work; it is very rich, but the ornament is much more judiciously arranged than in most edifices of a similar date.

WREXHAM CHURCH has a very fine tower, perhaps the finest in Wales; it is late, but good Perpendicular, very much enriched, the buttresses, full of niches, and the whole pannelled; the church is good, but not equal to the tower.

MOLD CHURCH is a good Perpendicular building, the tower modern.

NORTHOPE CHURCH has a fine plain tower, and some parts of the church are good.

GRESFORD CHURCH, near Wrexham, is small but very complete; the west walls, and part of the tower, appear to be Decorated, the rest Perpendicular in excellent preservation, and of good character; on the whole, a more complete little church is seldom met with, and its situation is very beautiful.

The church of FLINT, and that of CLYNOG near Caernarvon, may also be noticed.

In Wales, the architectural student should not neglect the castellated remains they are very numerous, and many of them contain very valuable specimens of castellated adaptations of the styles.

Scotland.

ROSLYN CHAPEL has already been mentioned for its singular composition.

The cathedrals of GLASGOW, DUMBLAINE, ABERDEEN, ELGIN, and that of ST. MAGNUS, at Kirkwall, in the island of Orkney, have all been magnificent structures, and though most of them are partially dilapidated, and variously altered, still contain enough to induce the student to a careful examination of their remains.

L

JEDBURG ABBEY has some fine Norman remains.

MELROSE ABBEY is in many respects the finest remain in Scotland; the Decorated portions are of very excellent character, and the tracery of the south transept window has seldom been exceeded. The eastern part is Perpendicular, and the east window has been a remarkably fine one, and one of which it is extremely difficult to restore the arrangement of the broken tracery.

The chapel of HOLYROOD PALACE, though in ruins, has some good work.

Ireland.

The CATHEDRAL of ST. PATRICK, in Dublin, is the only building the Author can with confidence refer to; this is mostly of Early English character, with various introductions and alterations. No doubt the island contains other edifices worthy of attention, though they have not as yet come under the Author's notice.

FINIS.

J. and J. Smith, Printers, Liverpool.

For EU product safety concerns, contact us at Calle de José Abascal, 56–1°,
28003 Madrid, Spain or eugpsr@cambridge.org.

www.ingramcontent.com/pod-product-compliance
Ingram Content Group UK Ltd.
Pitfield, Milton Keynes, MK11 3LW, UK
UKHW012341130625
459647UK00009B/449